THE PICTURE BOOK OF

CATS

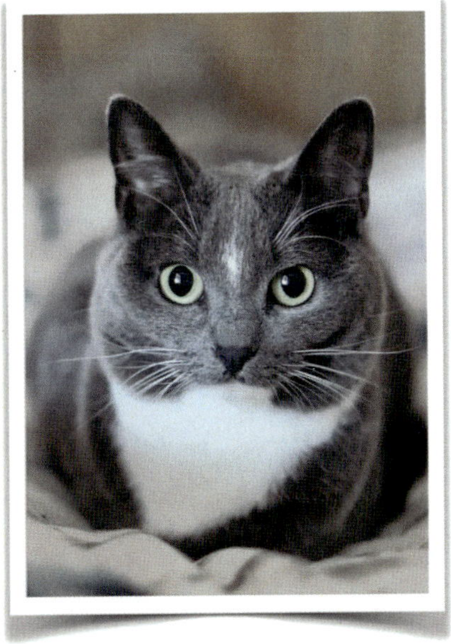

SUNNY STREET
BOOKS

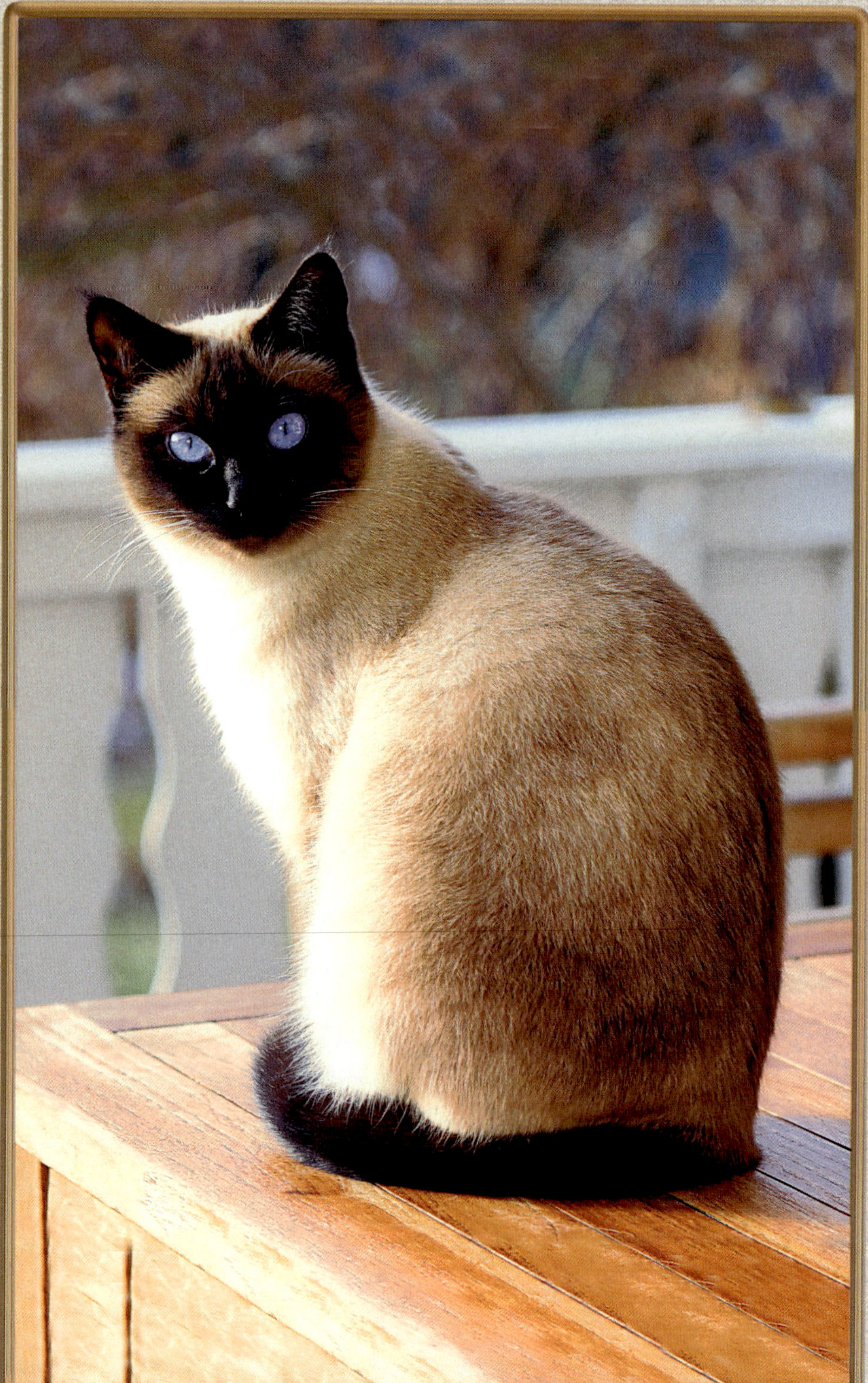

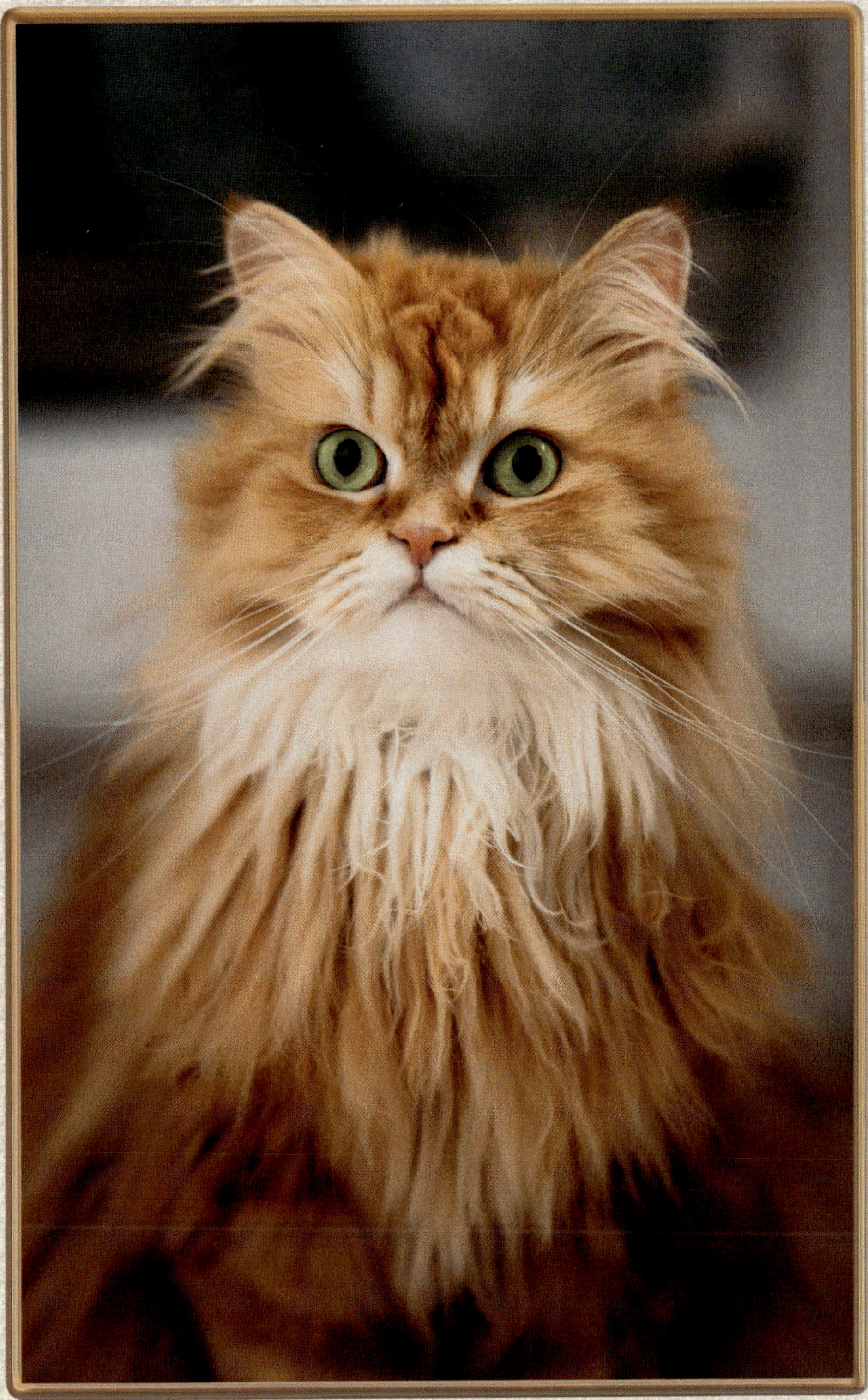

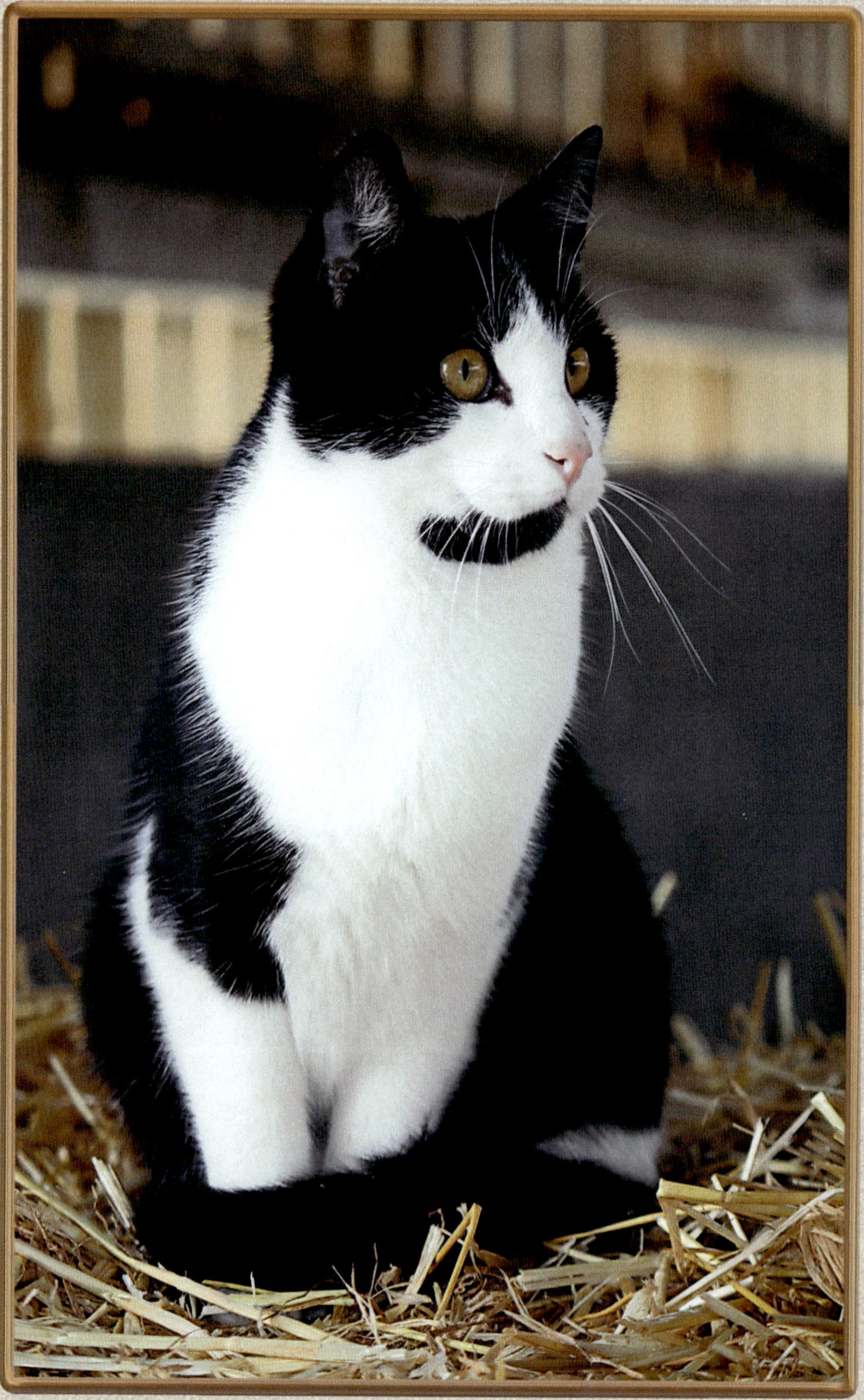

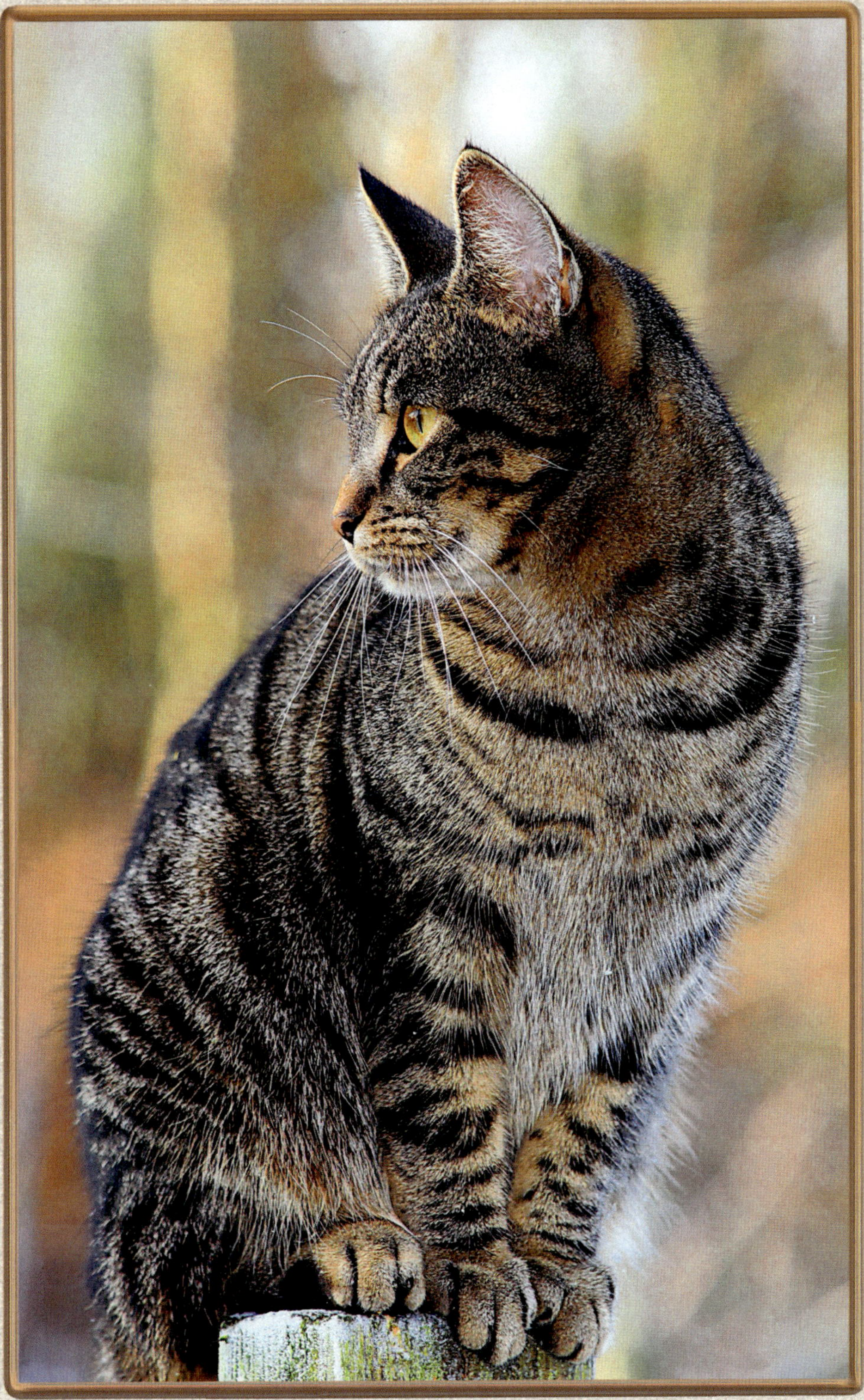

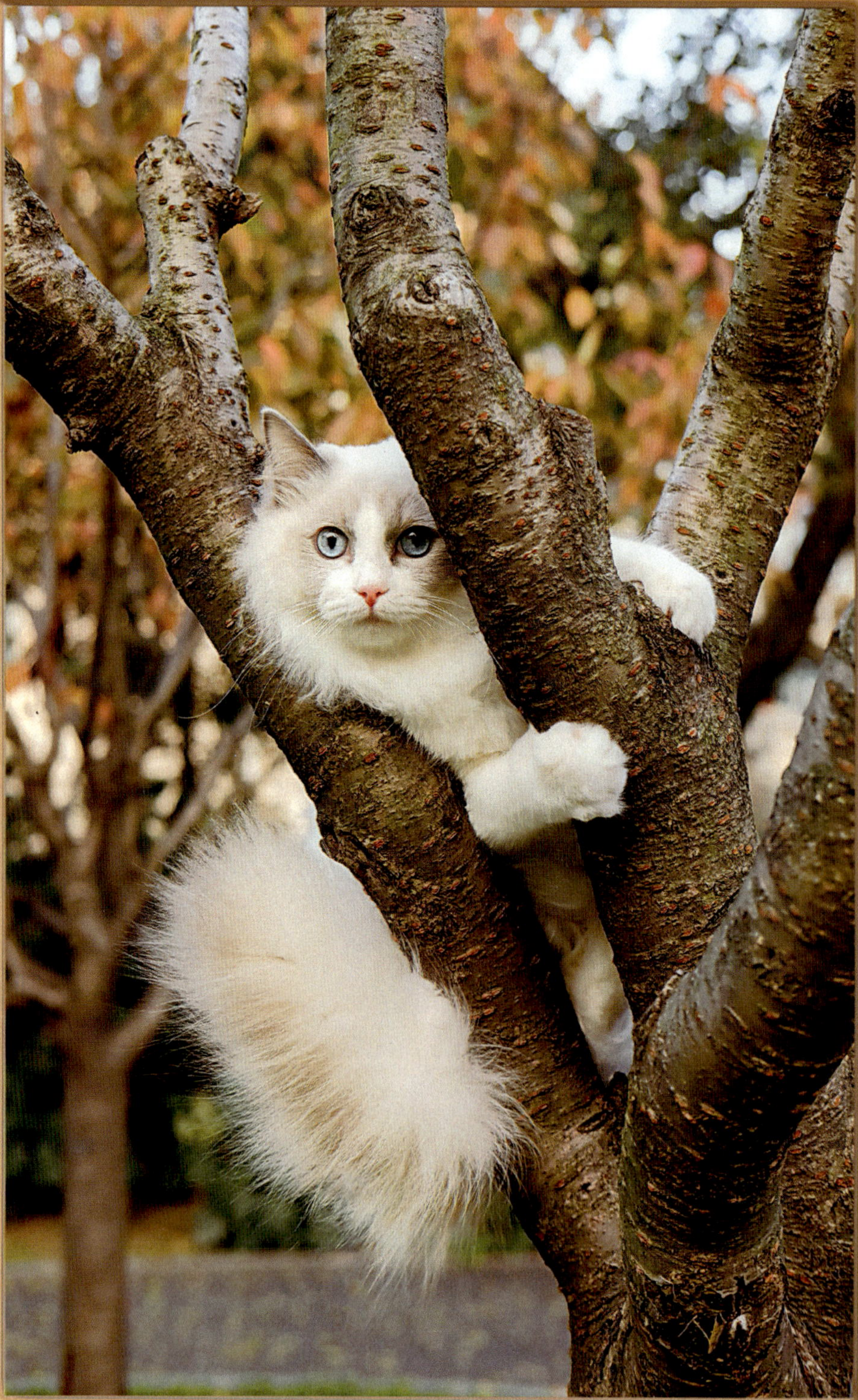

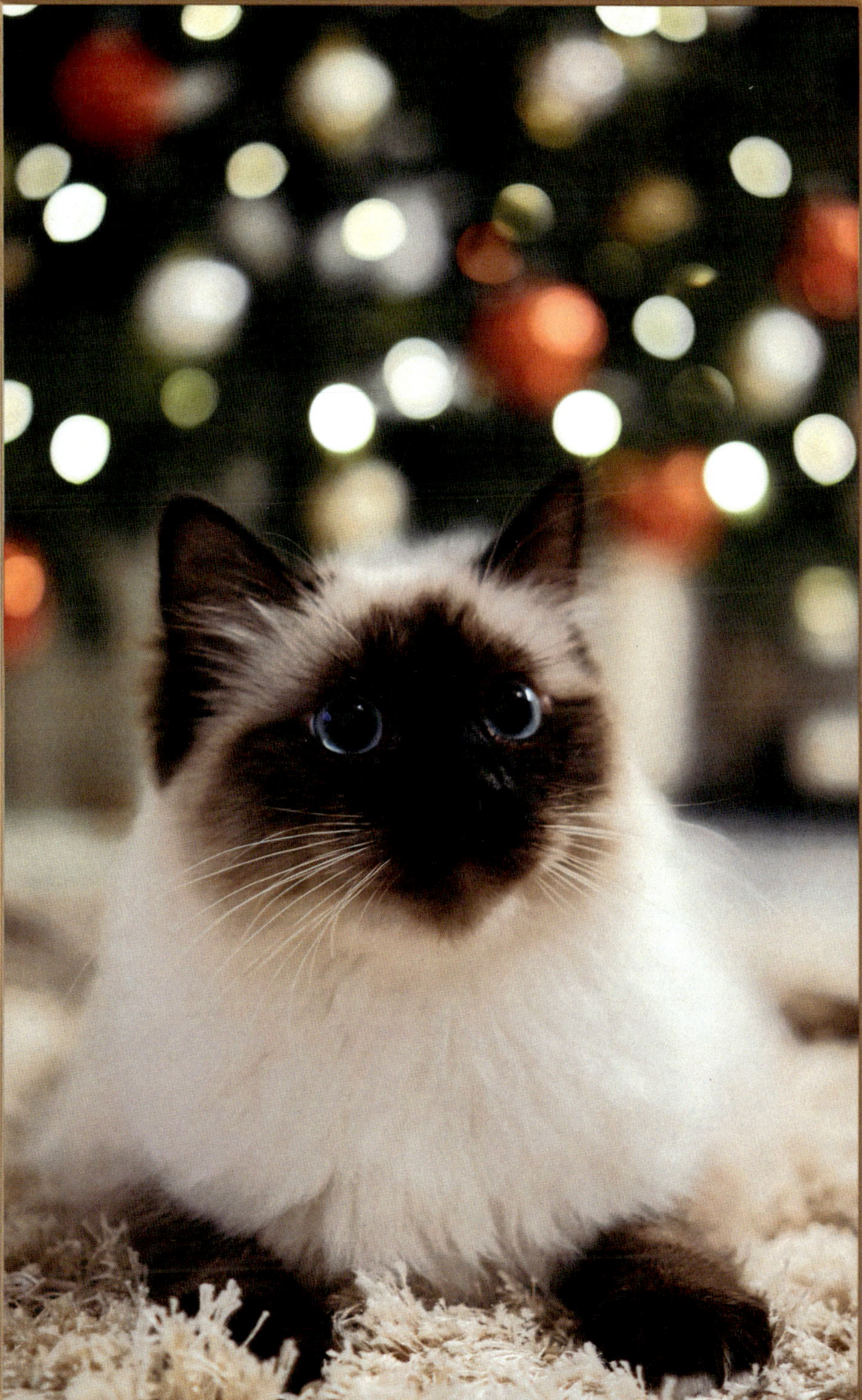

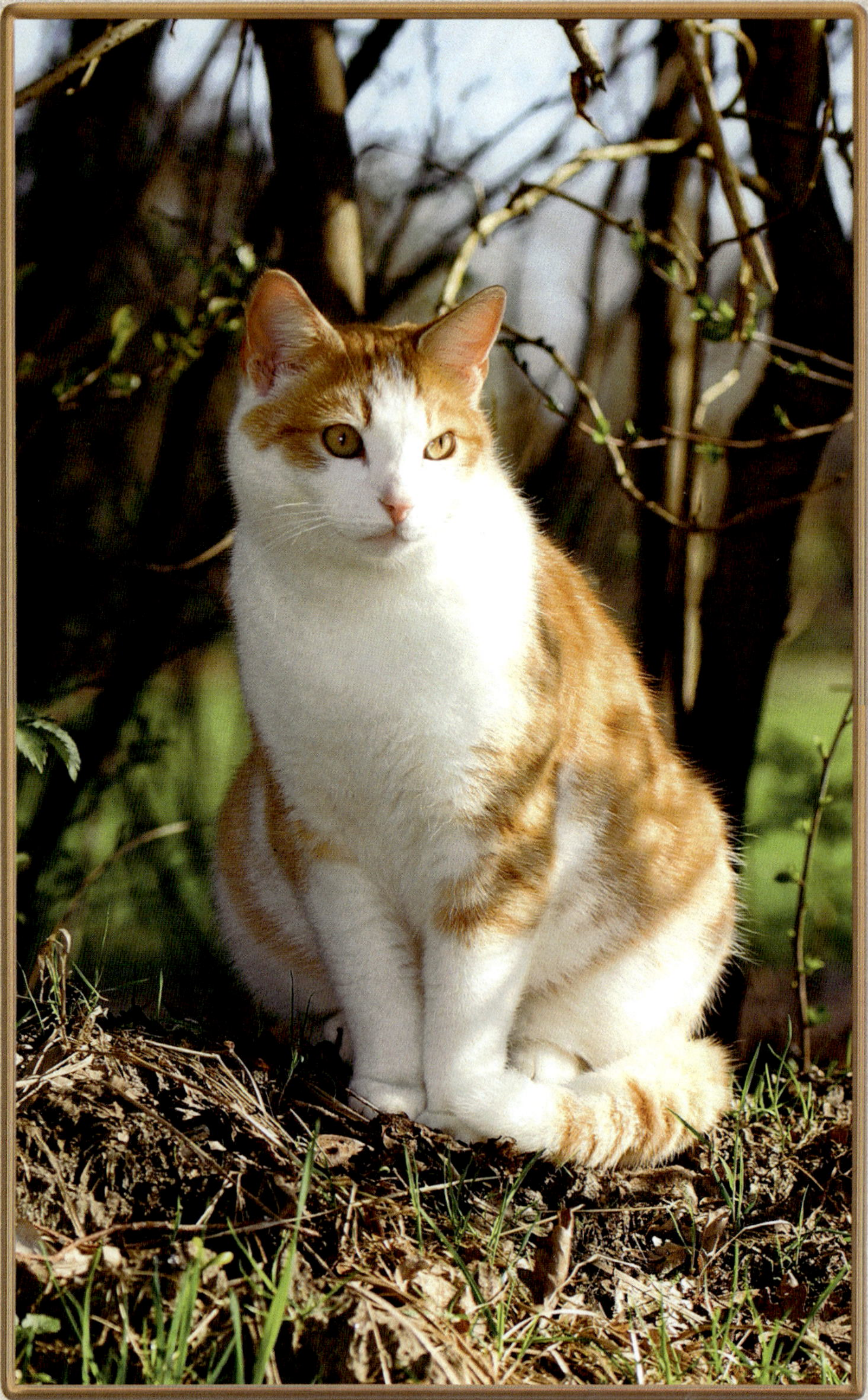

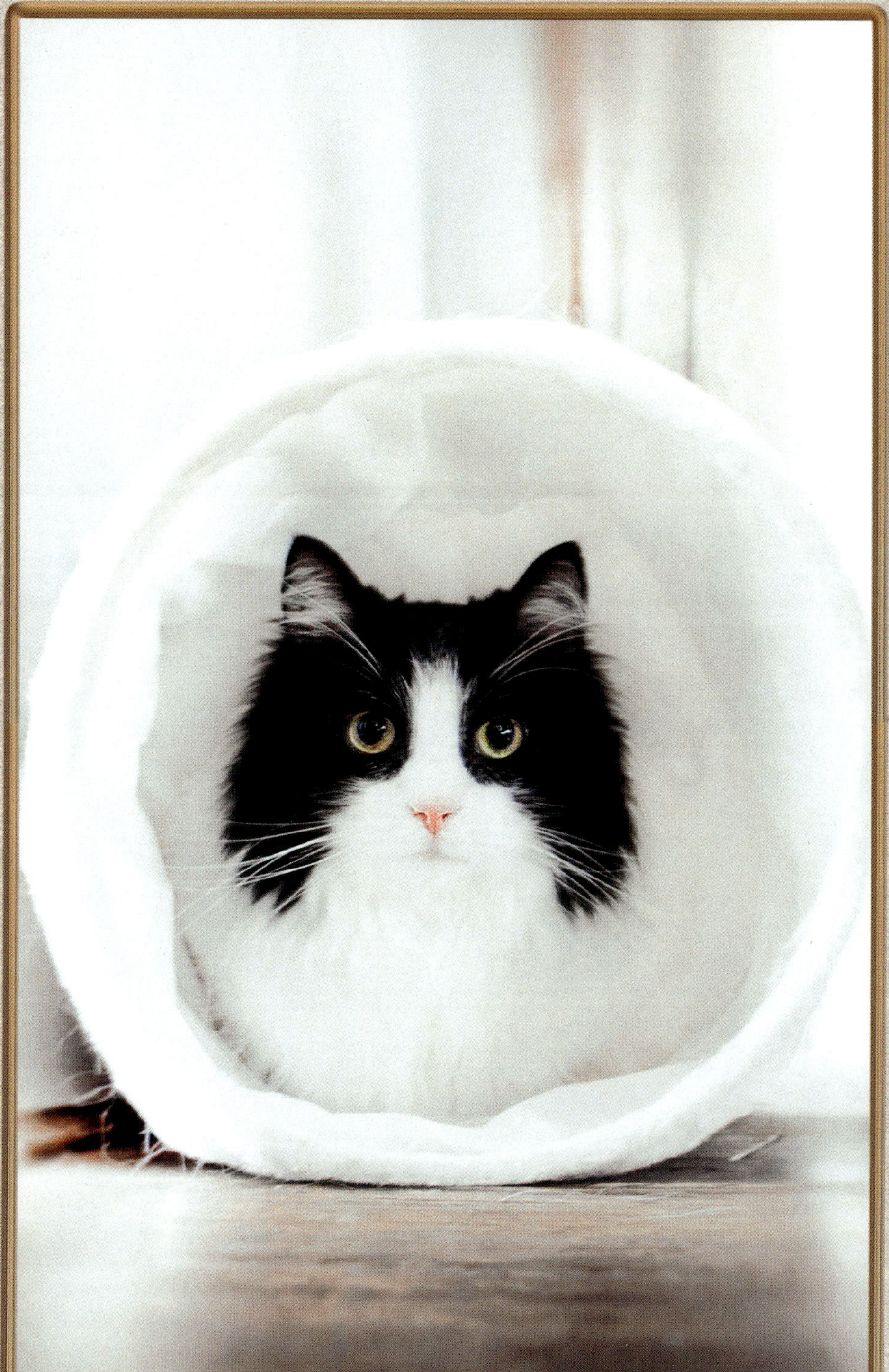

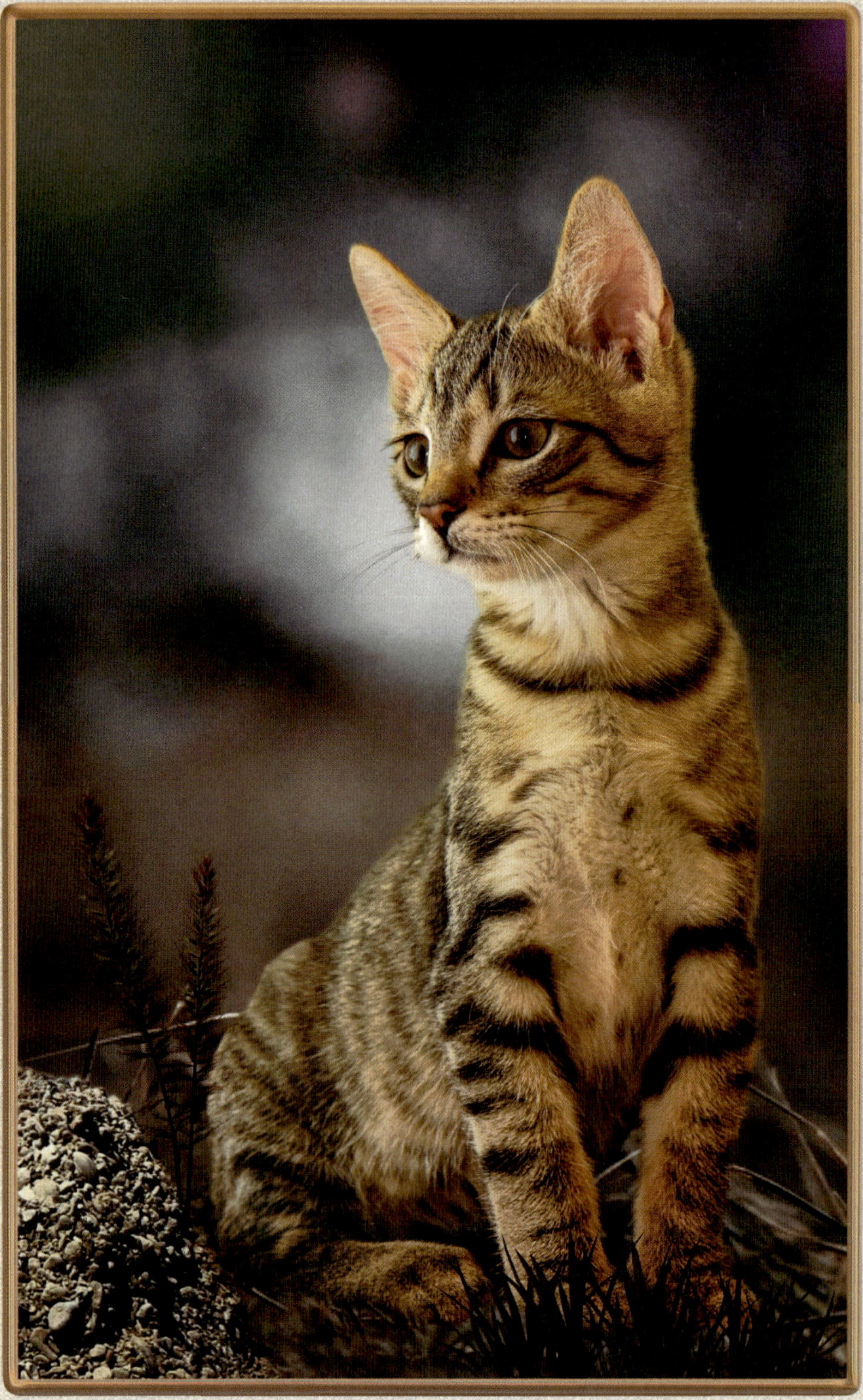

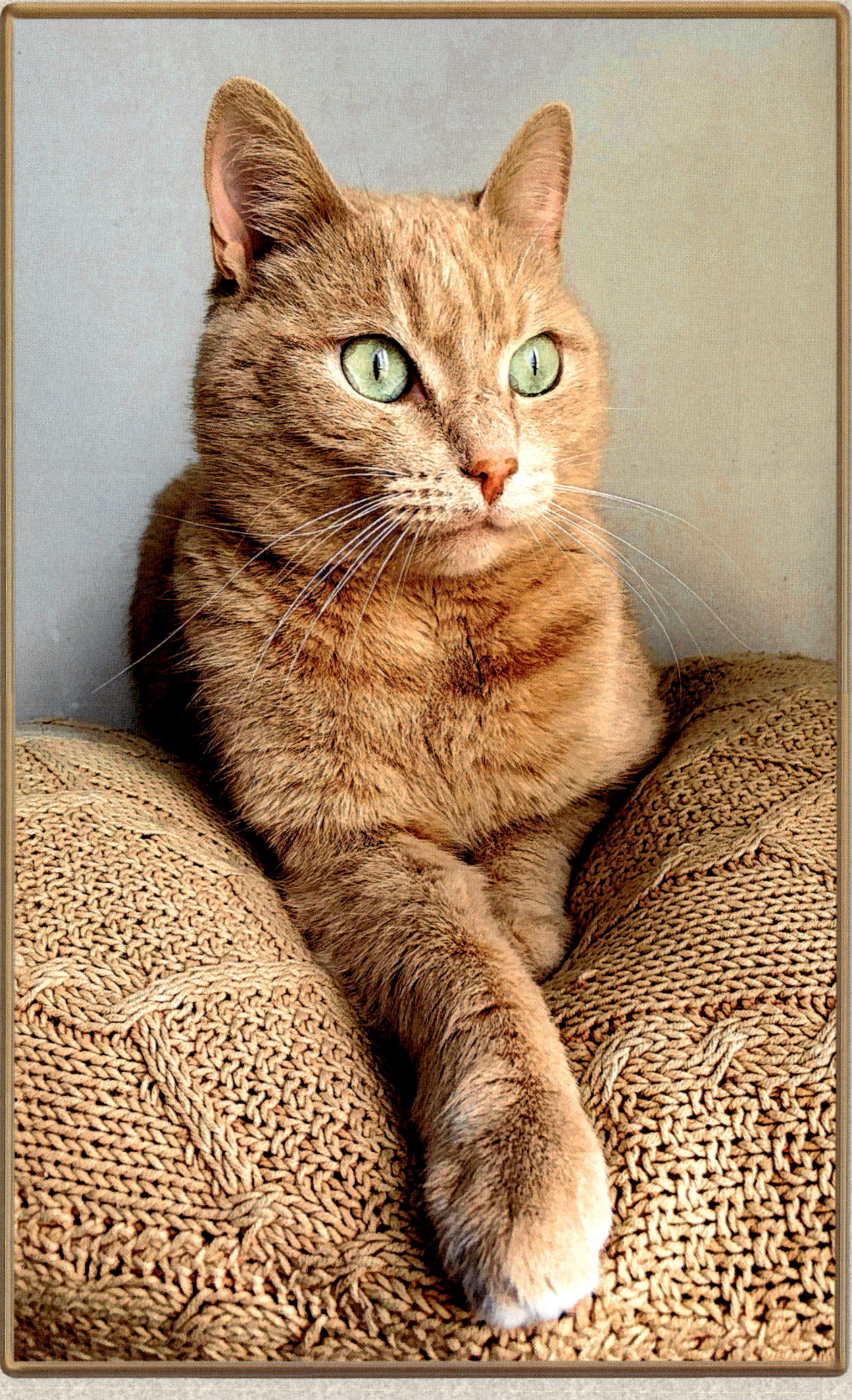

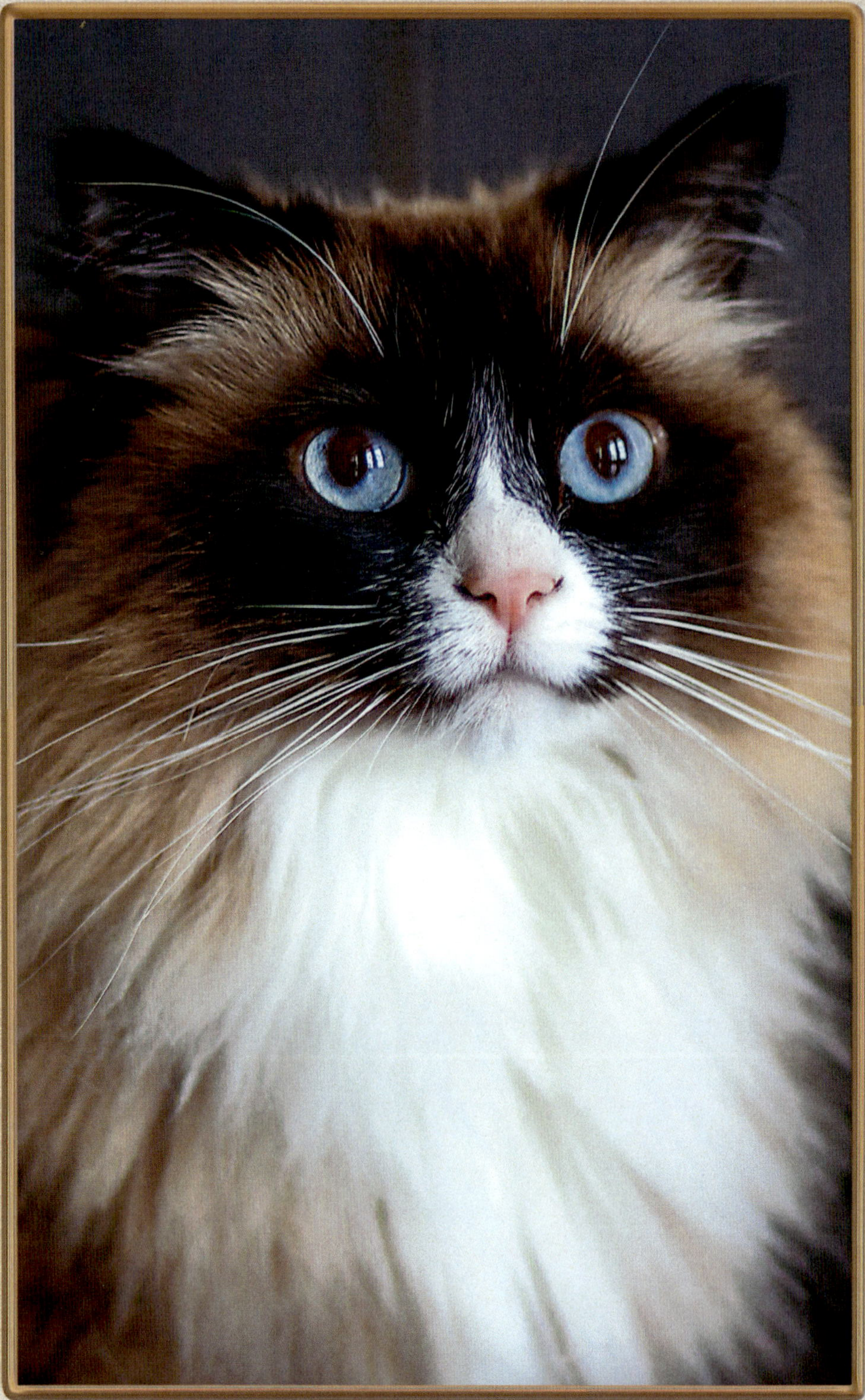

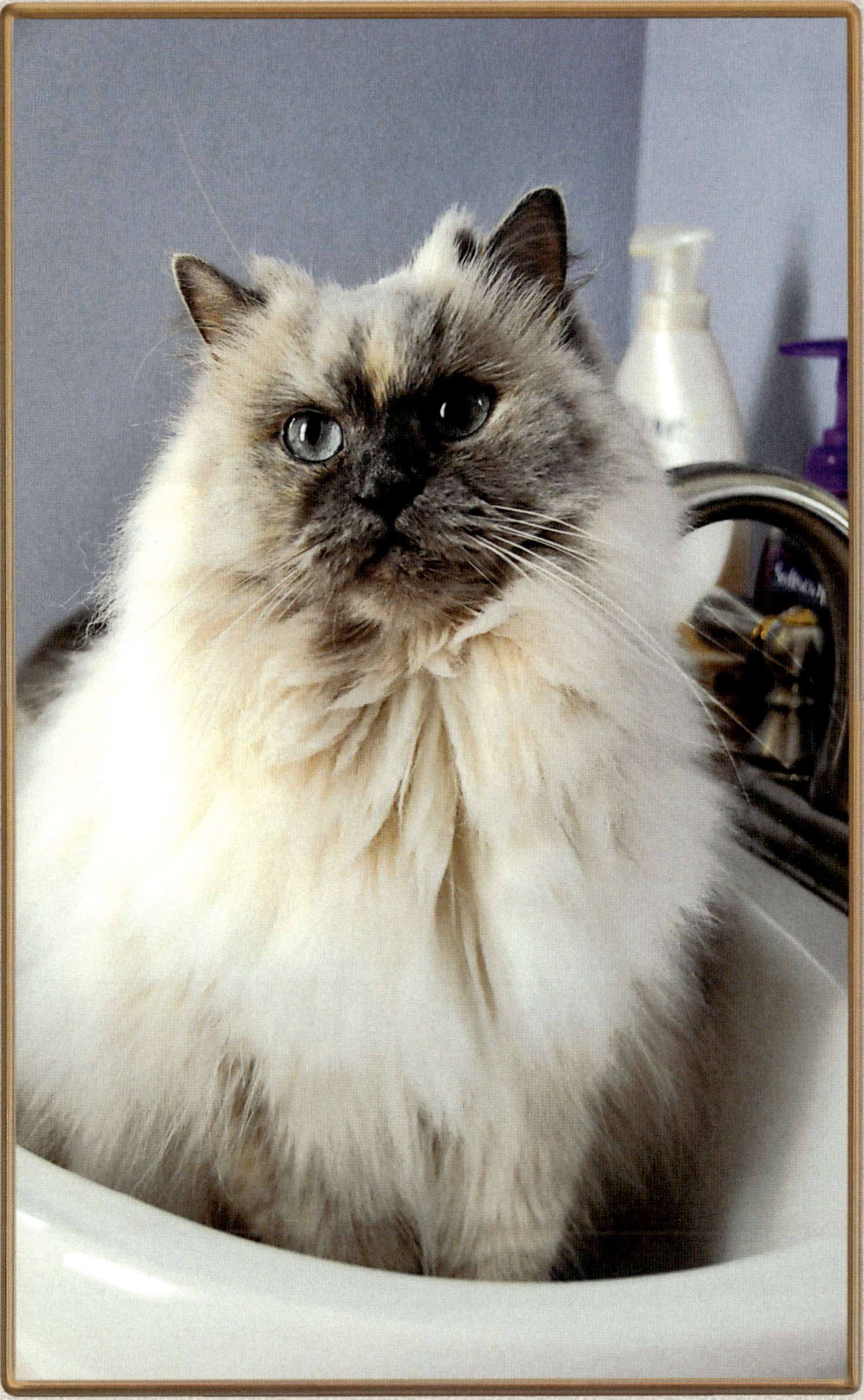

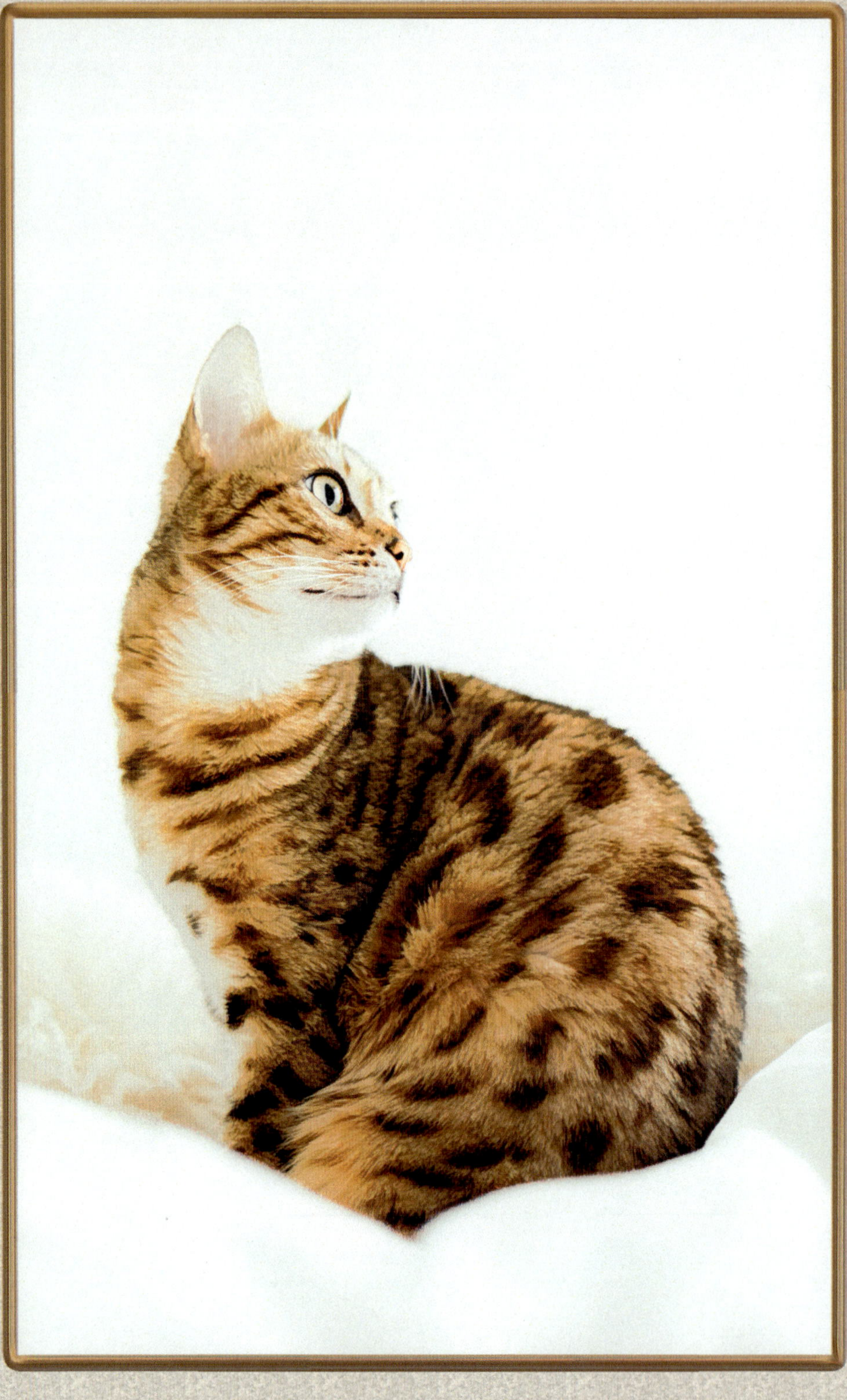

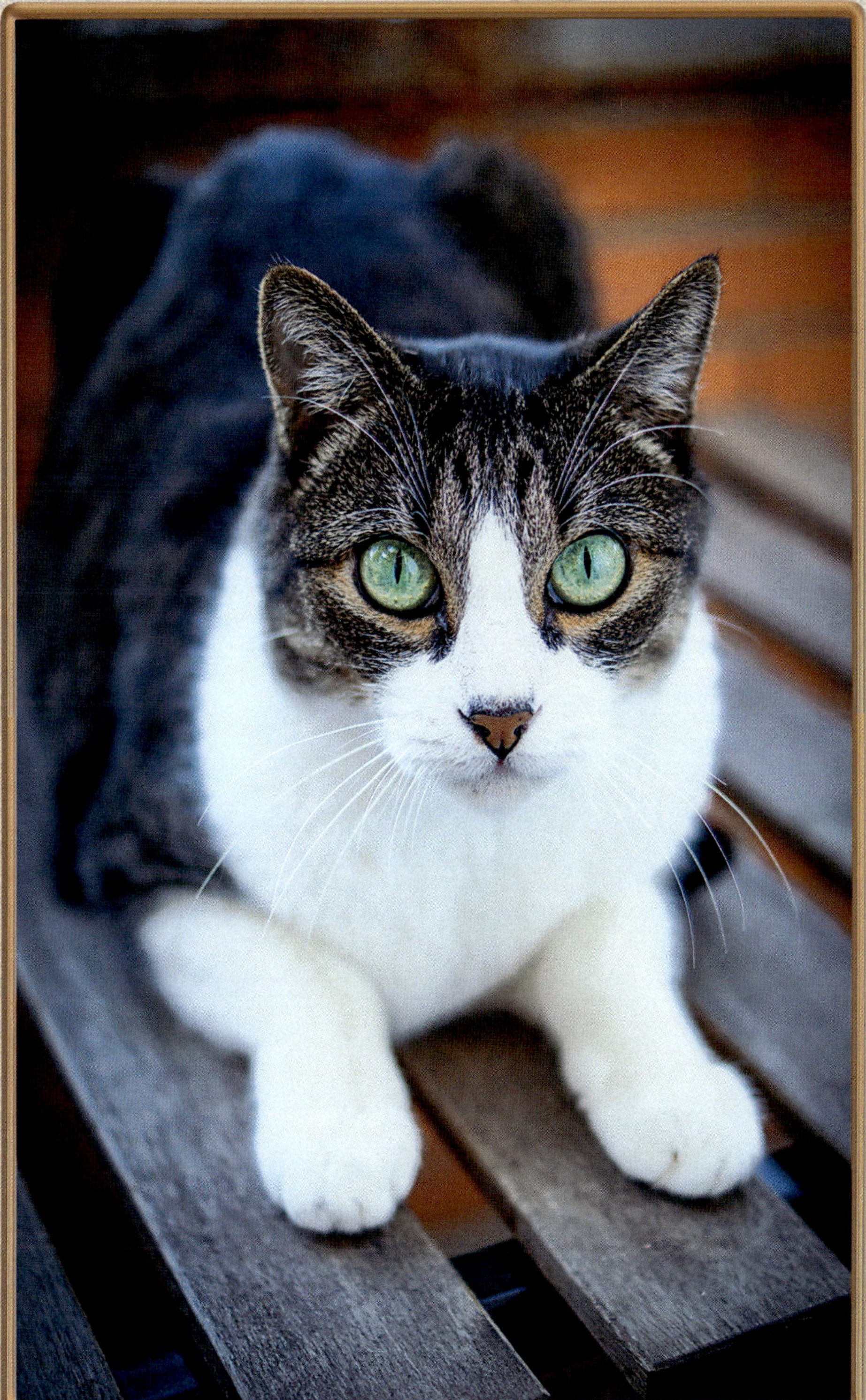

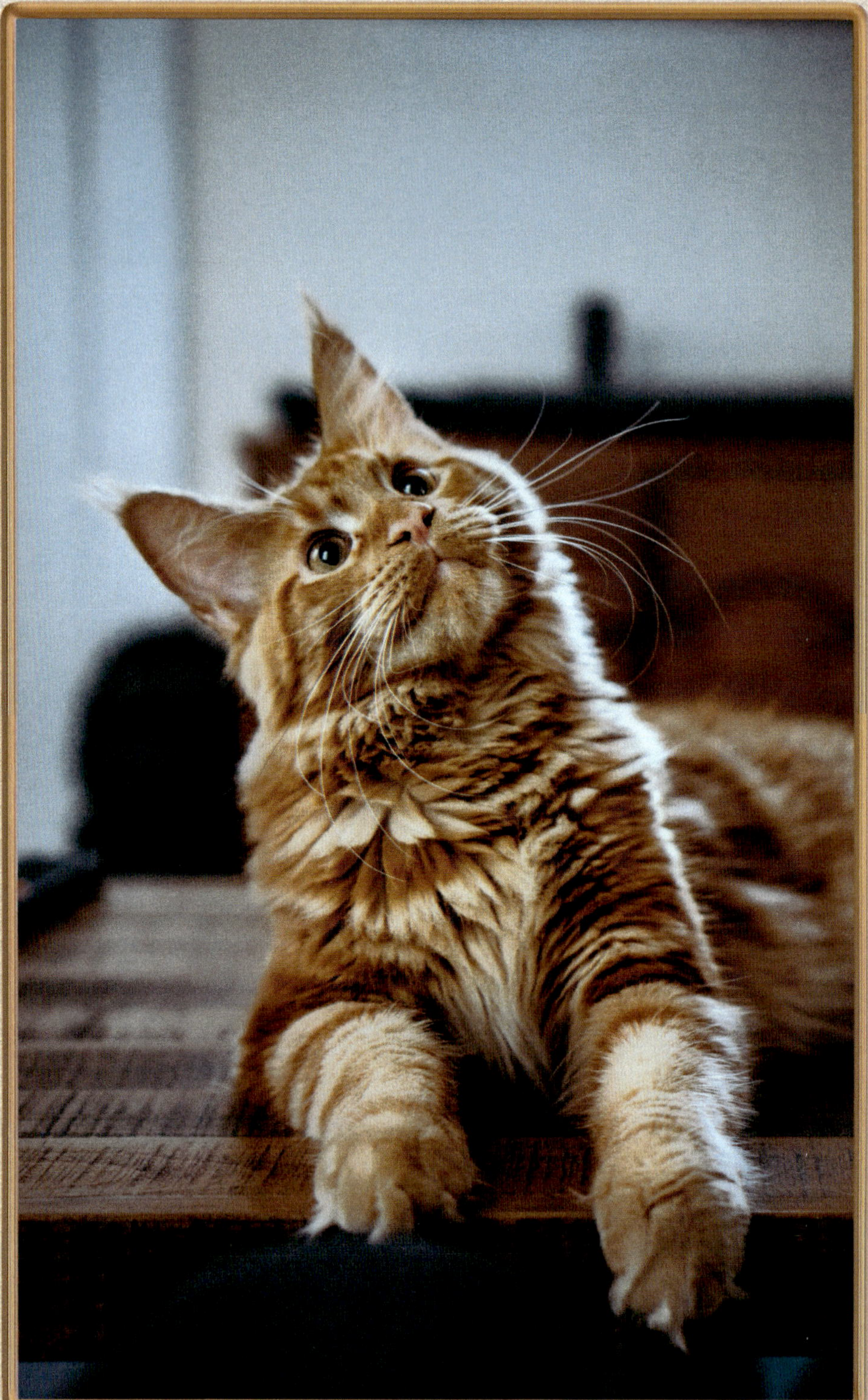

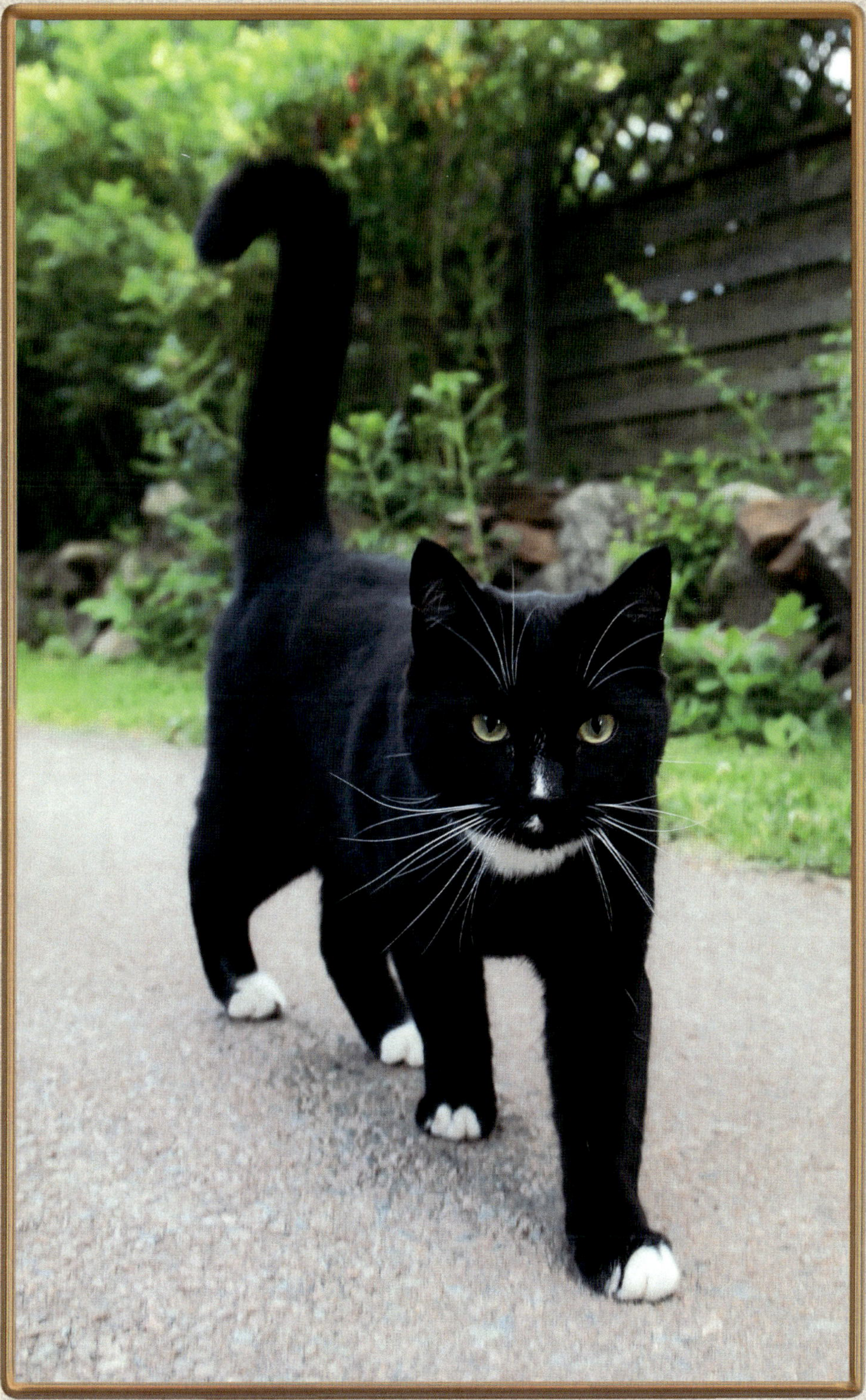

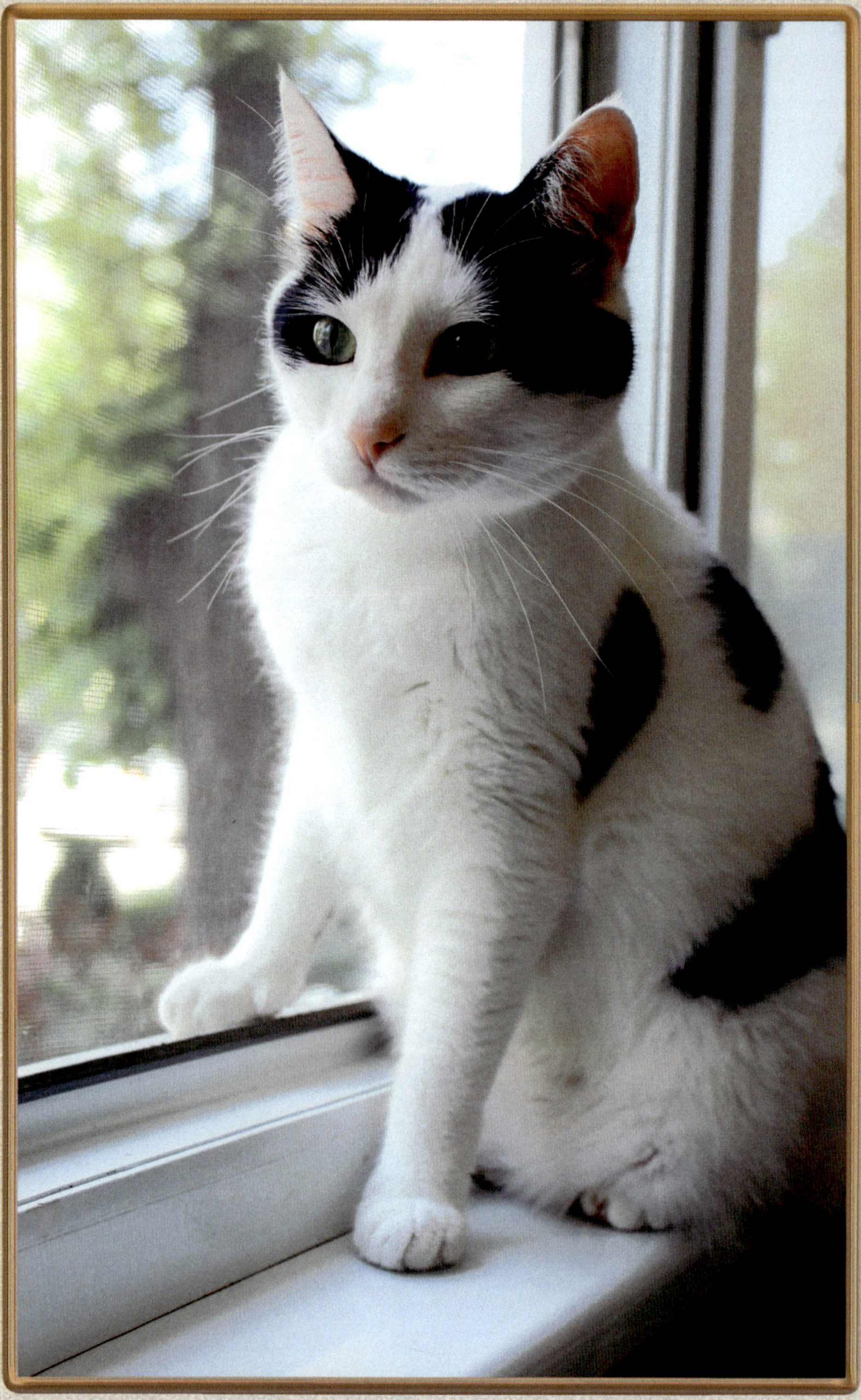

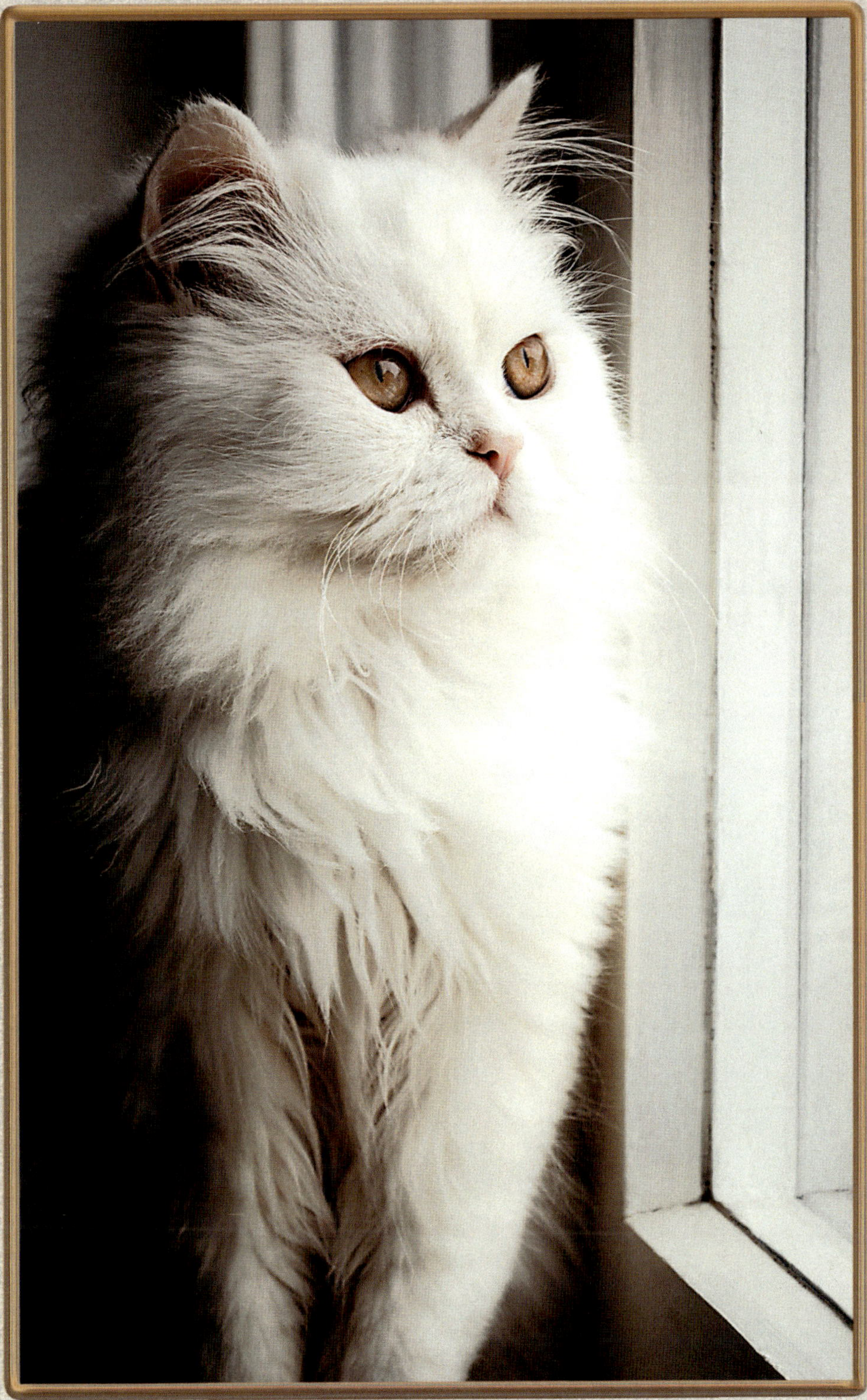

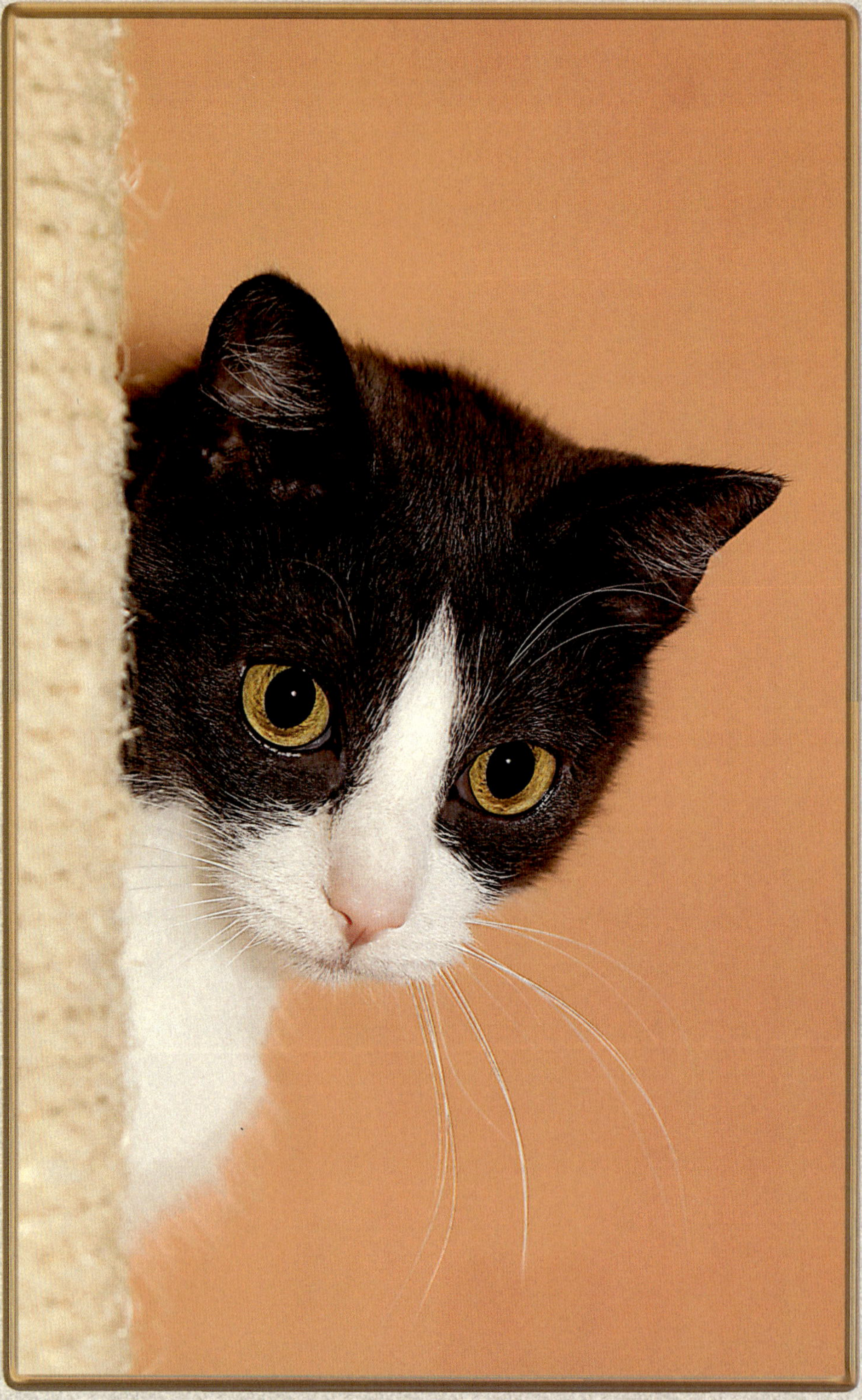

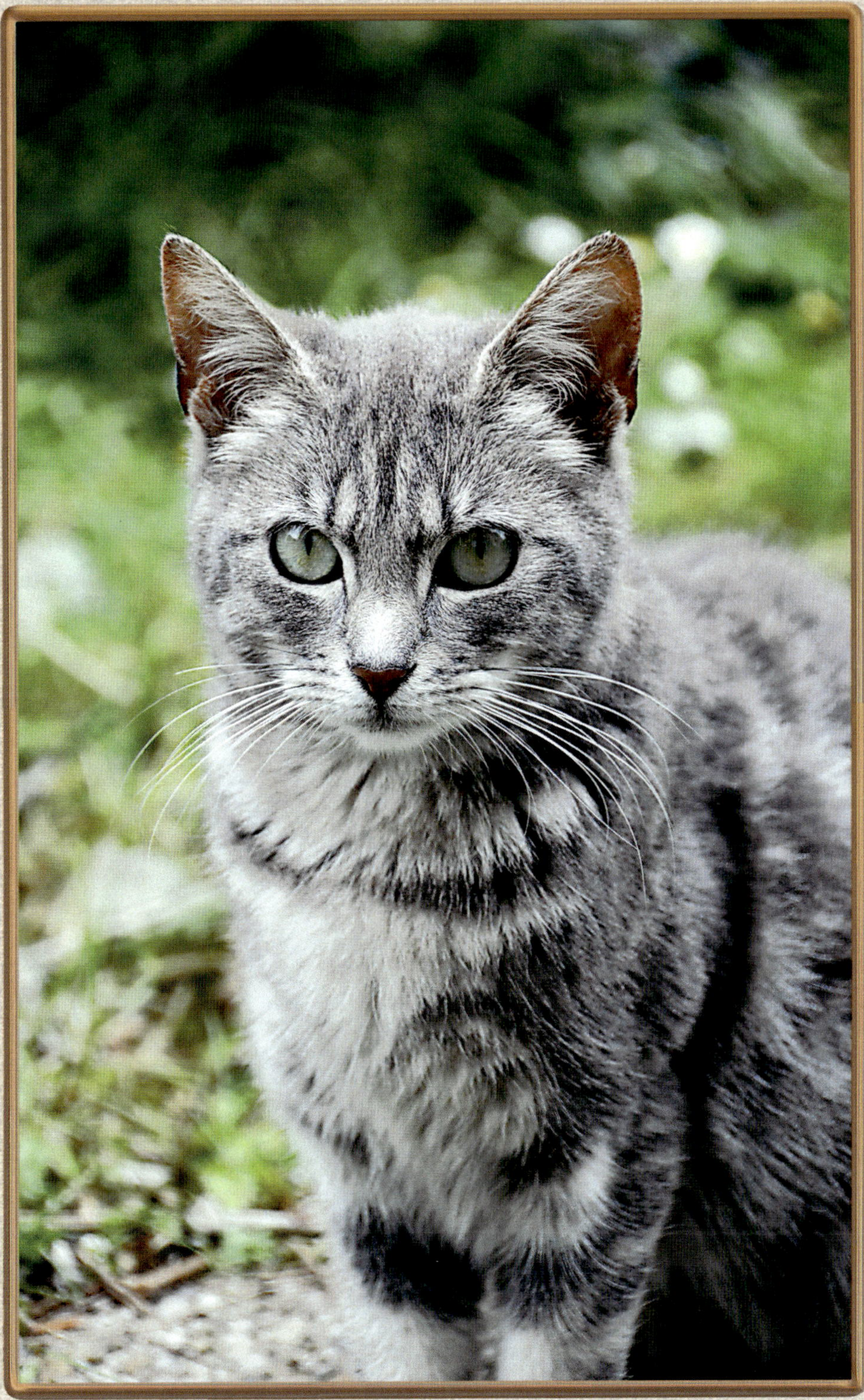

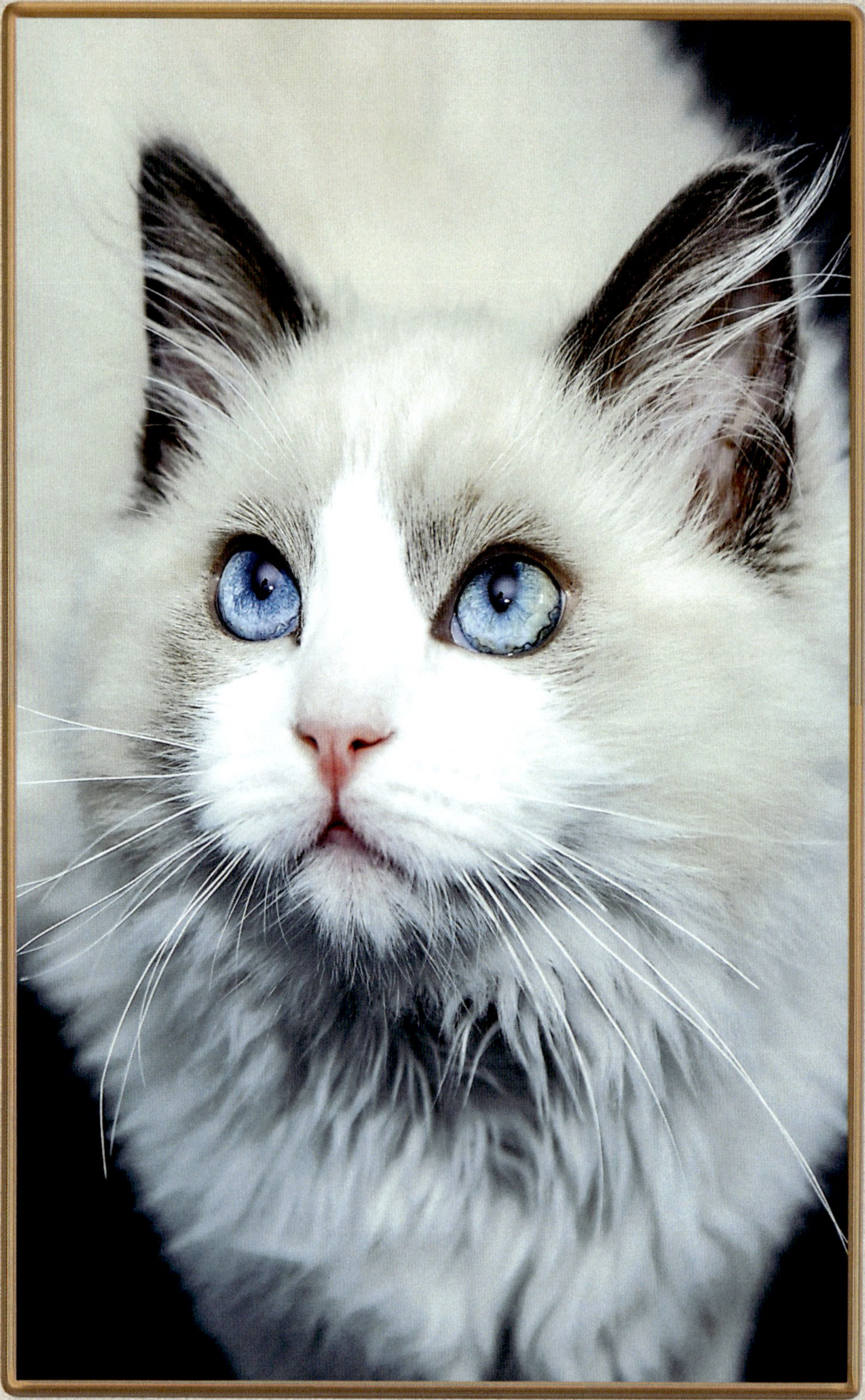

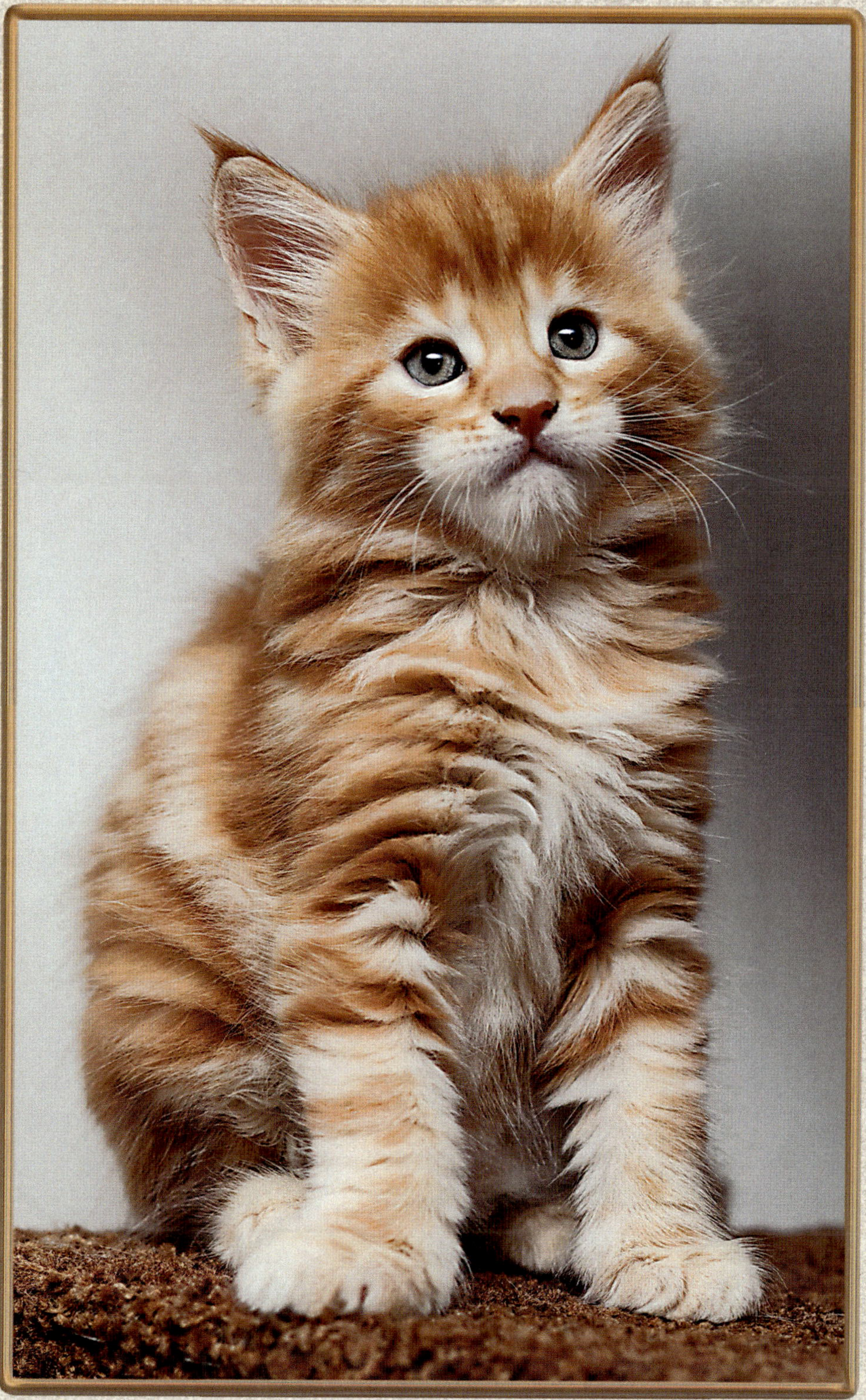

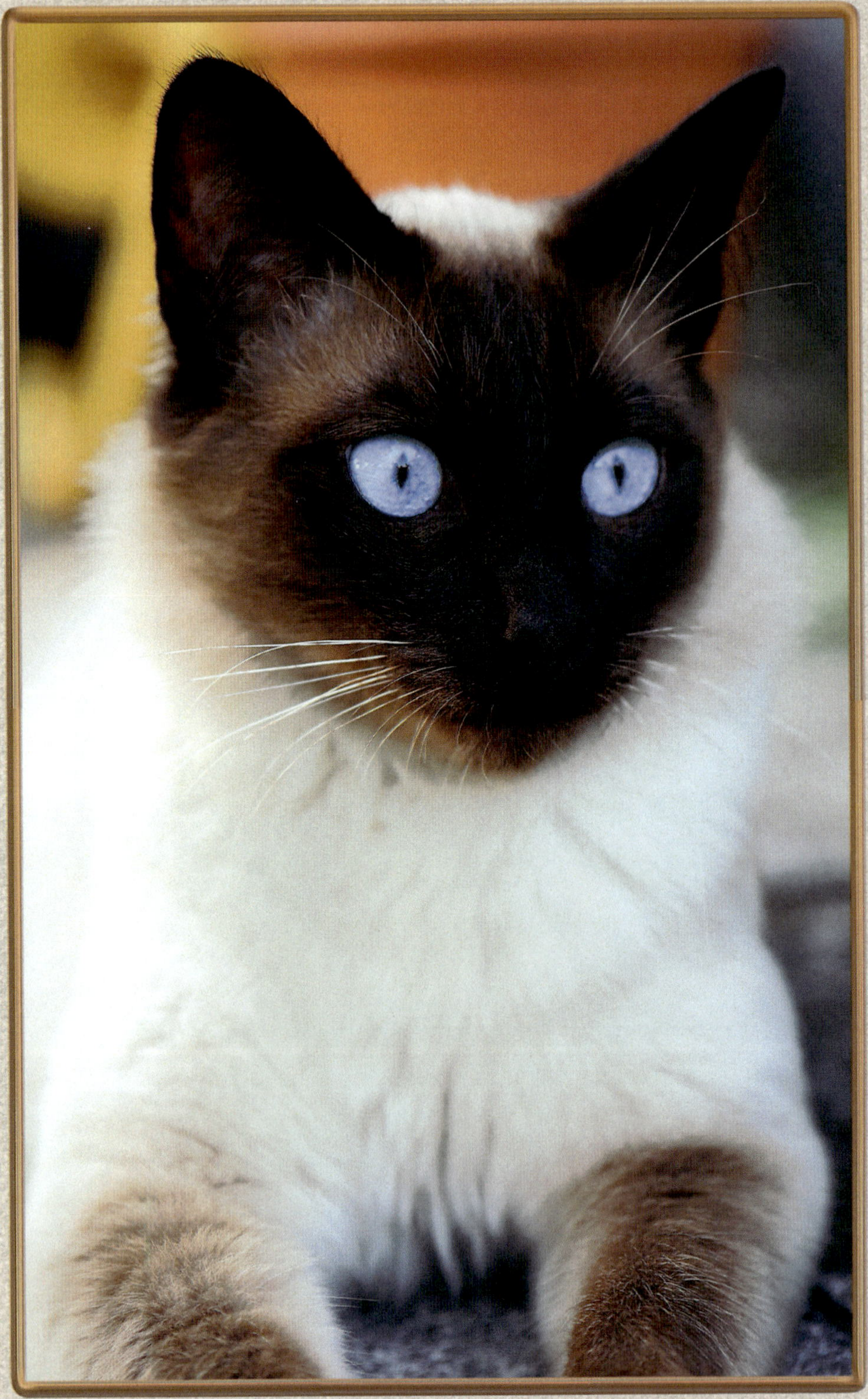

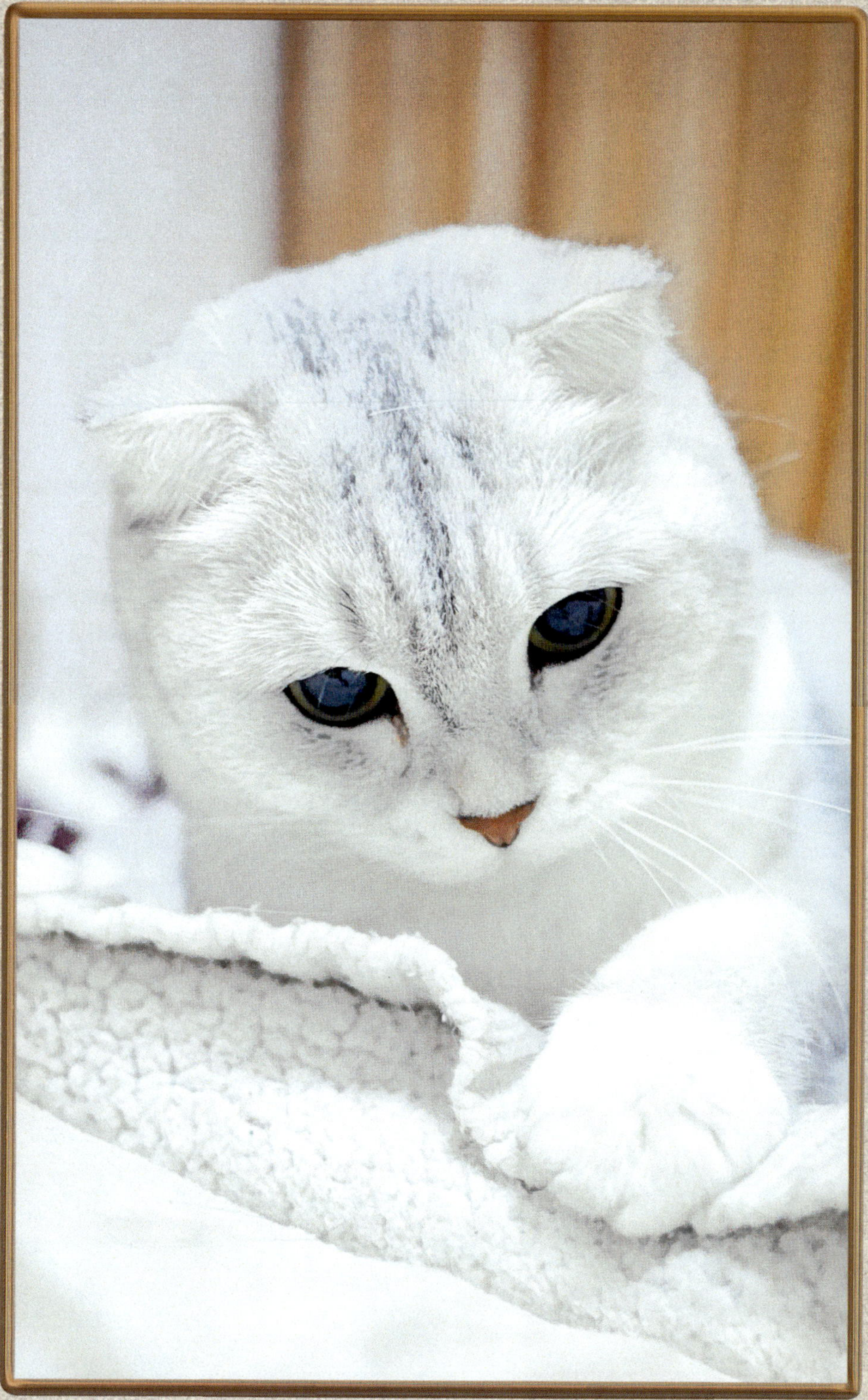

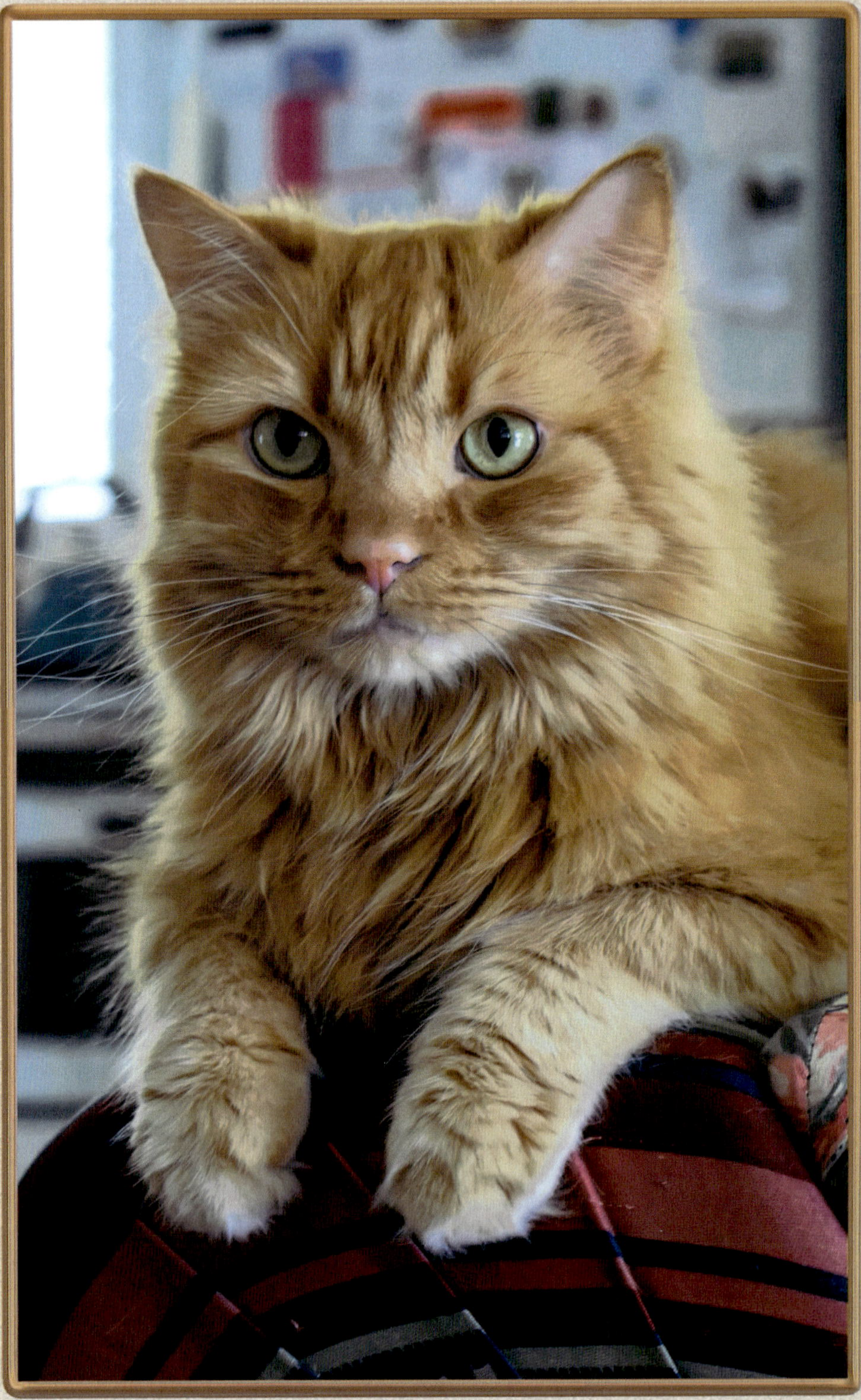

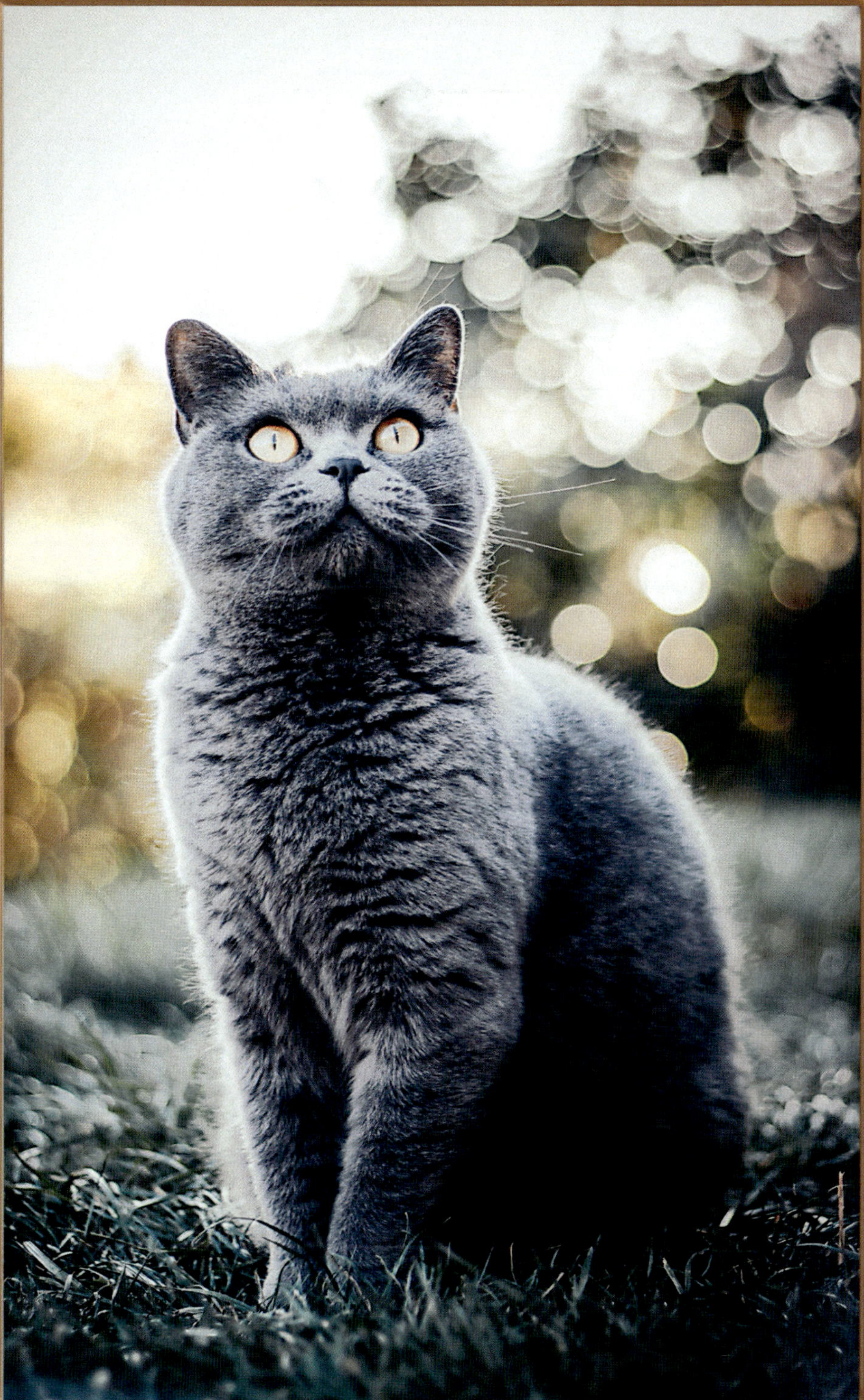

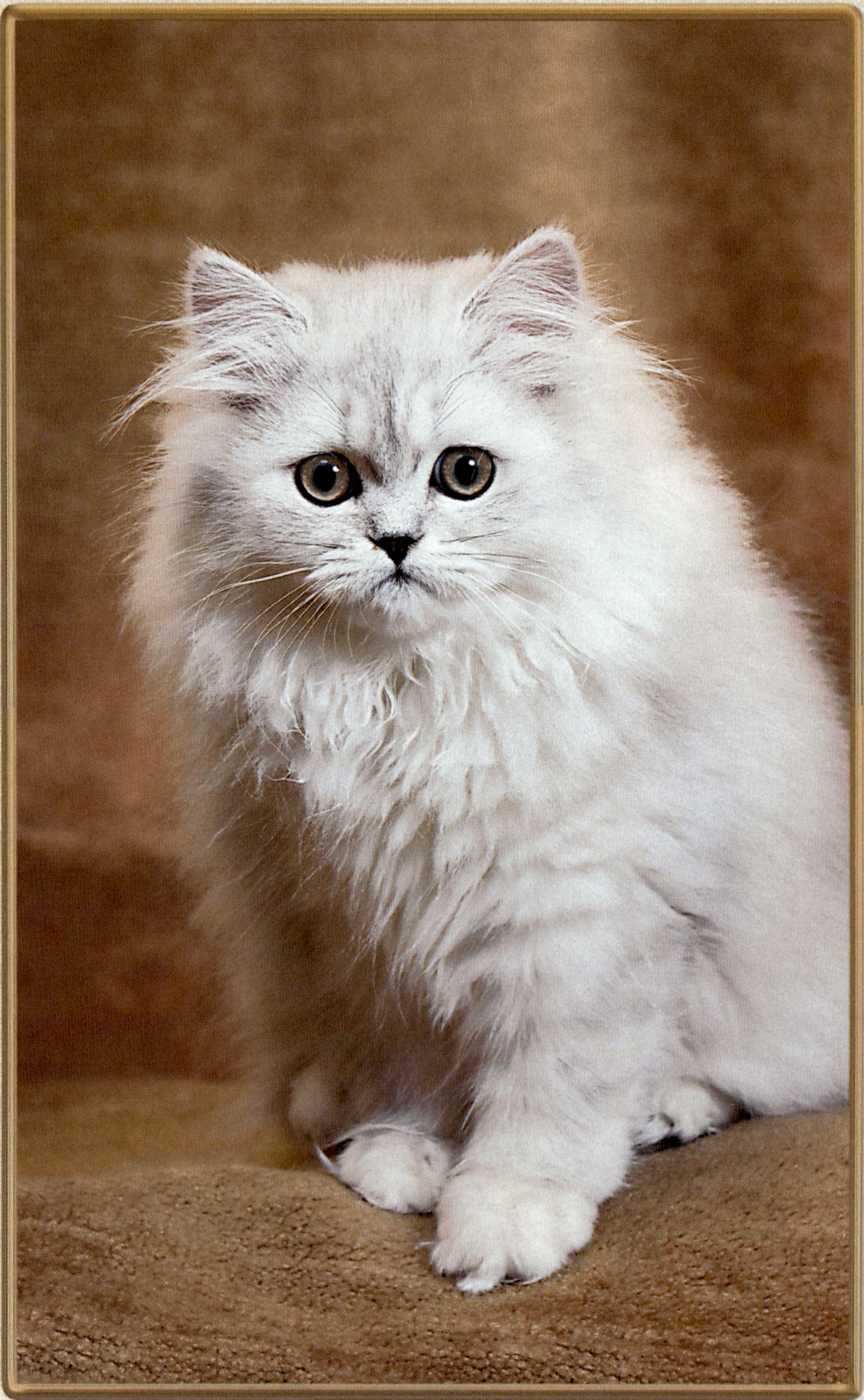

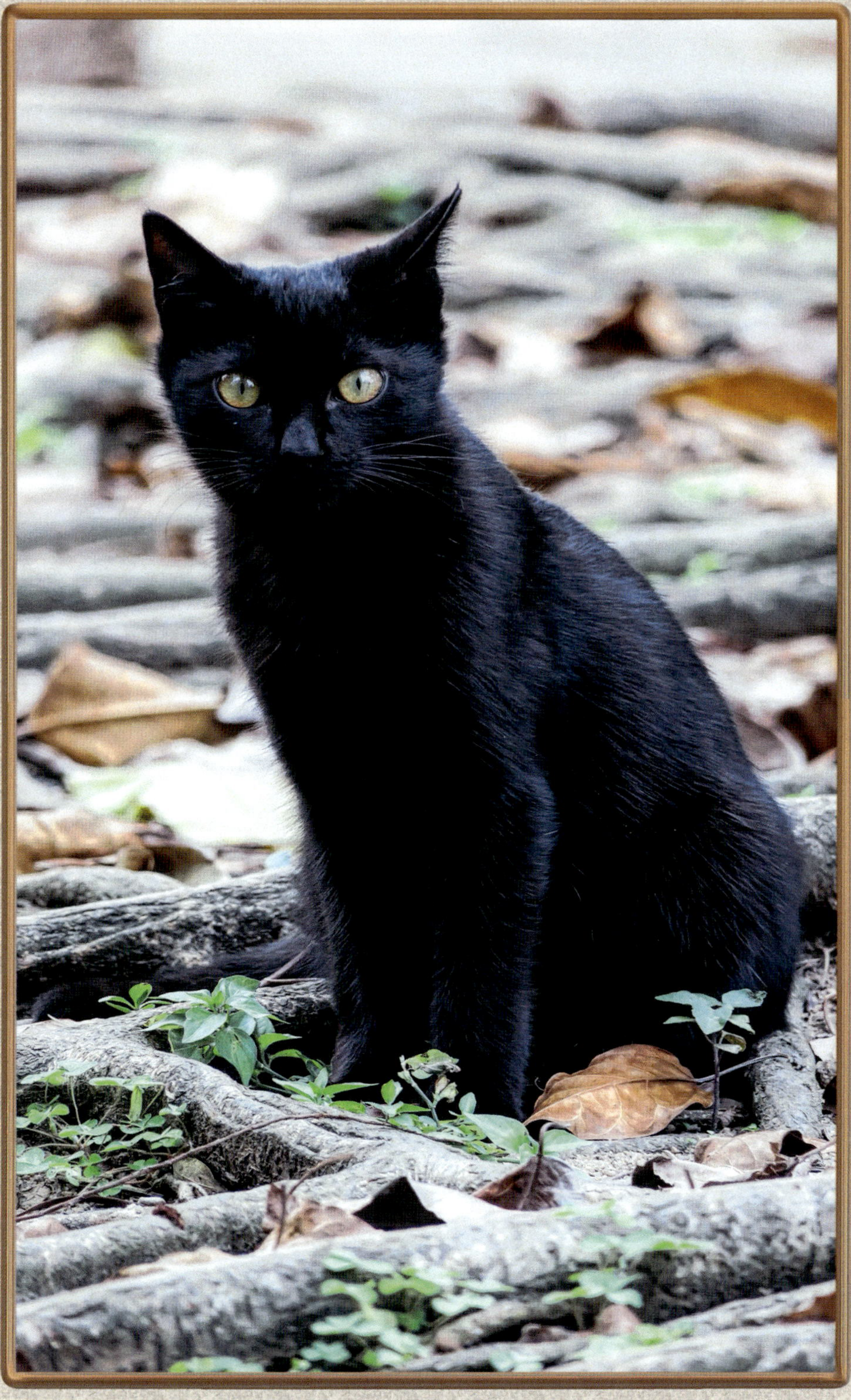

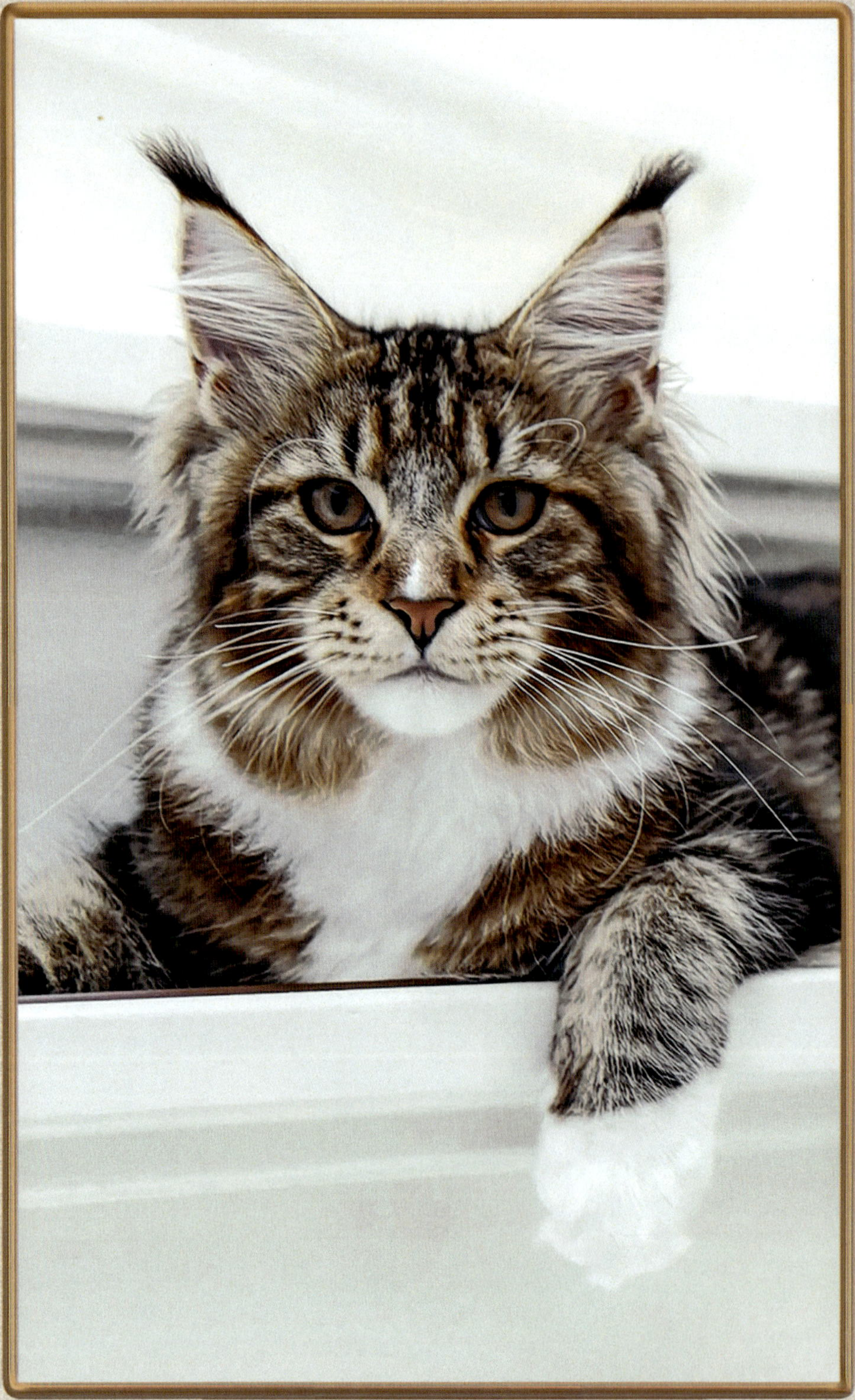

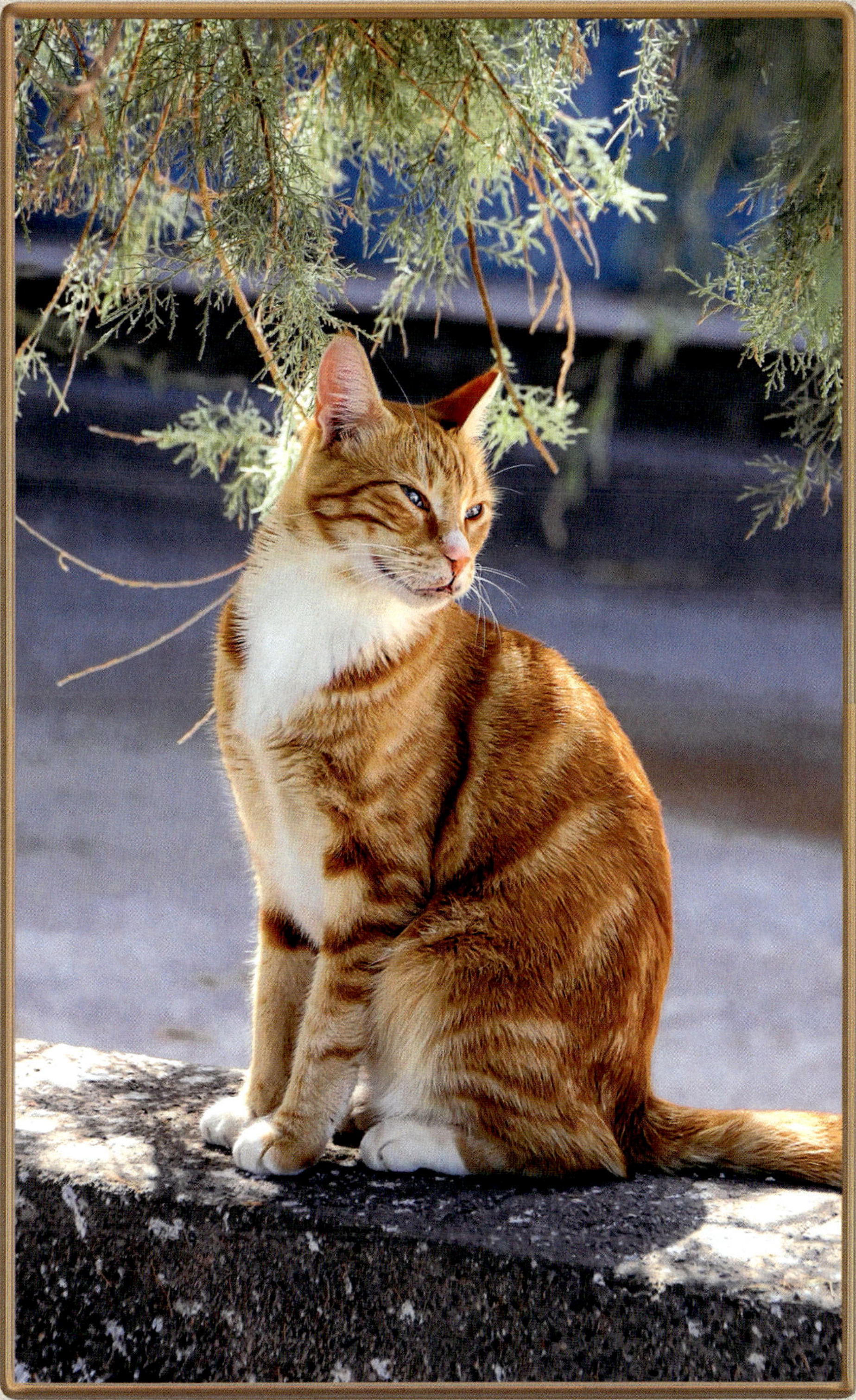

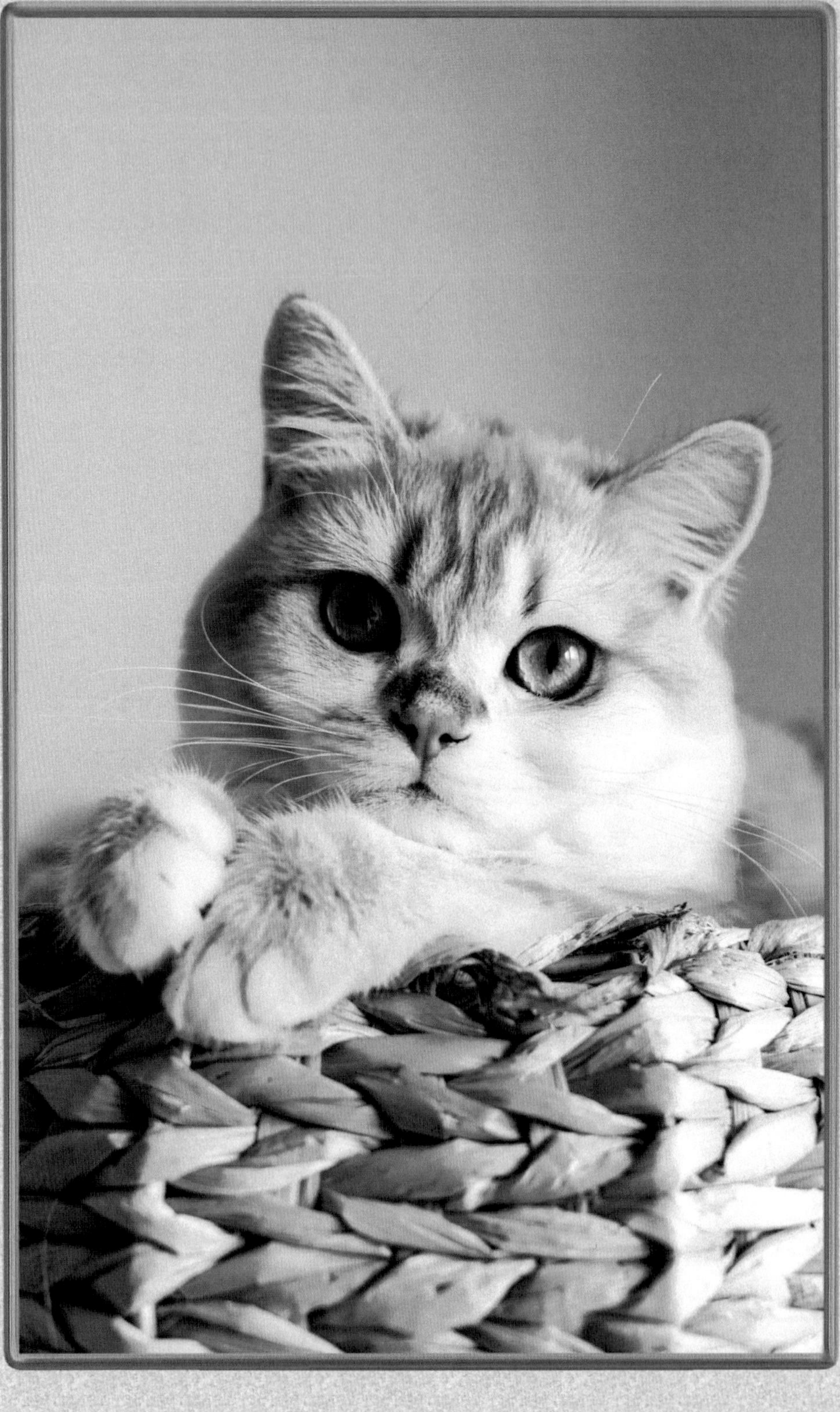

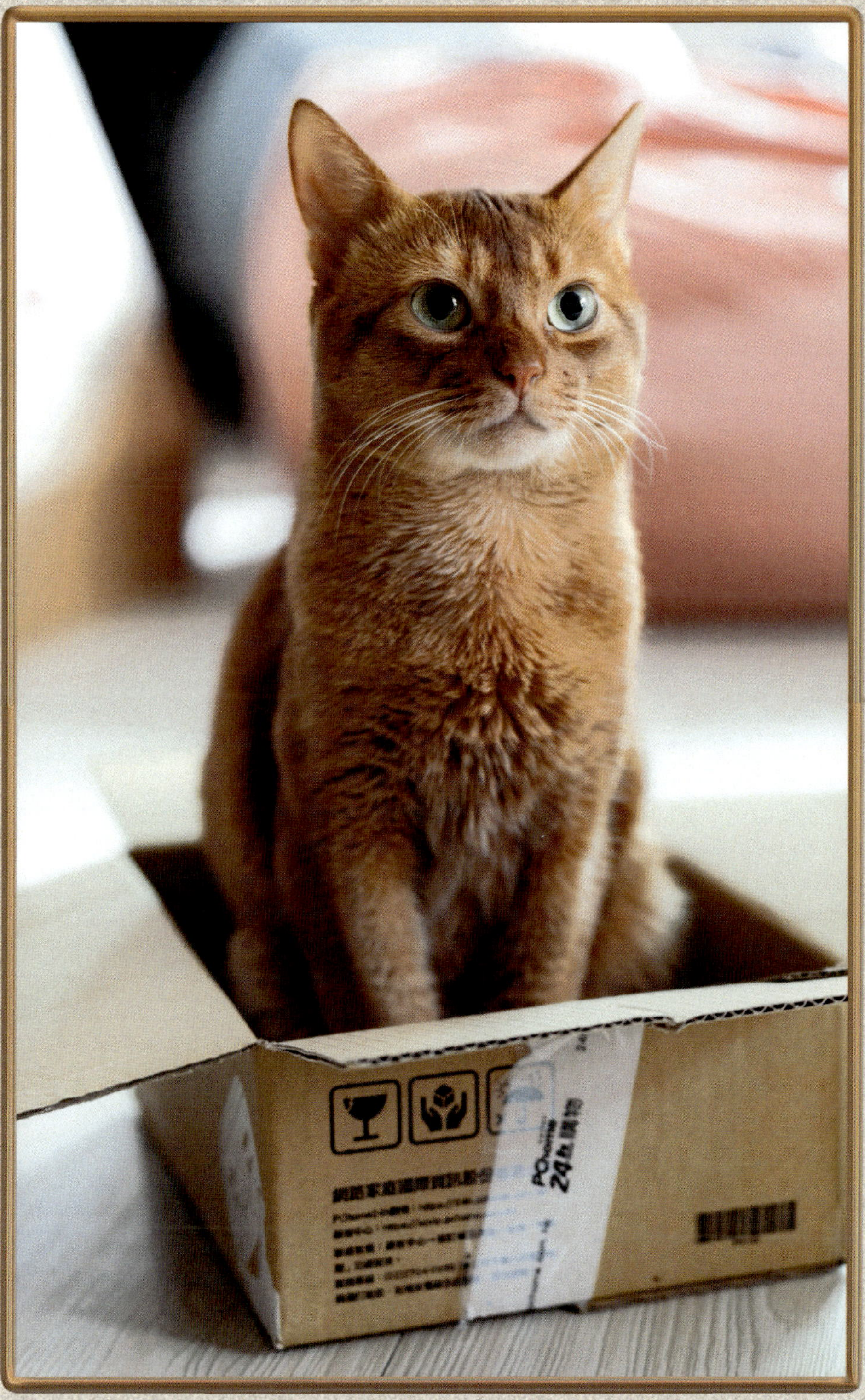

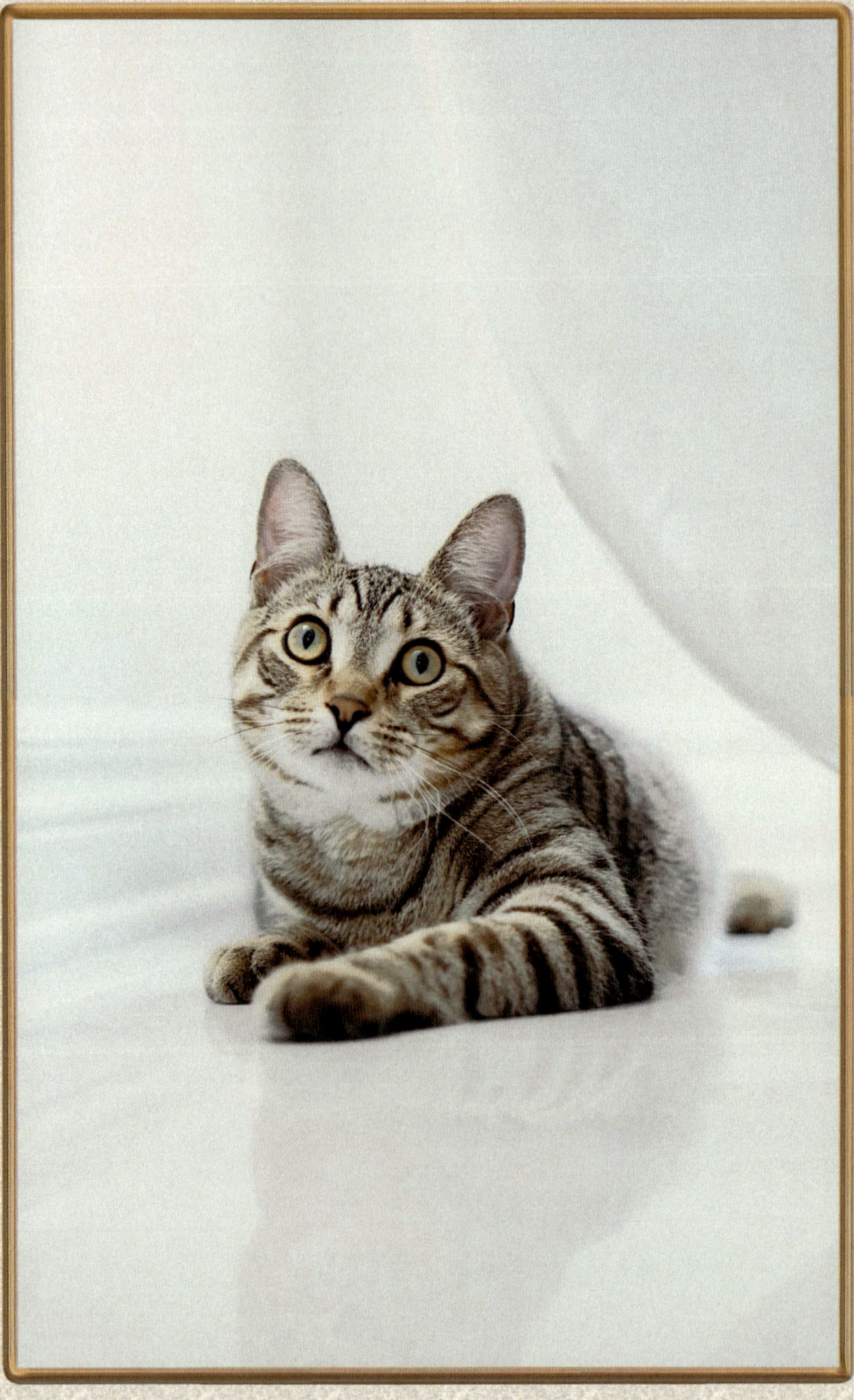

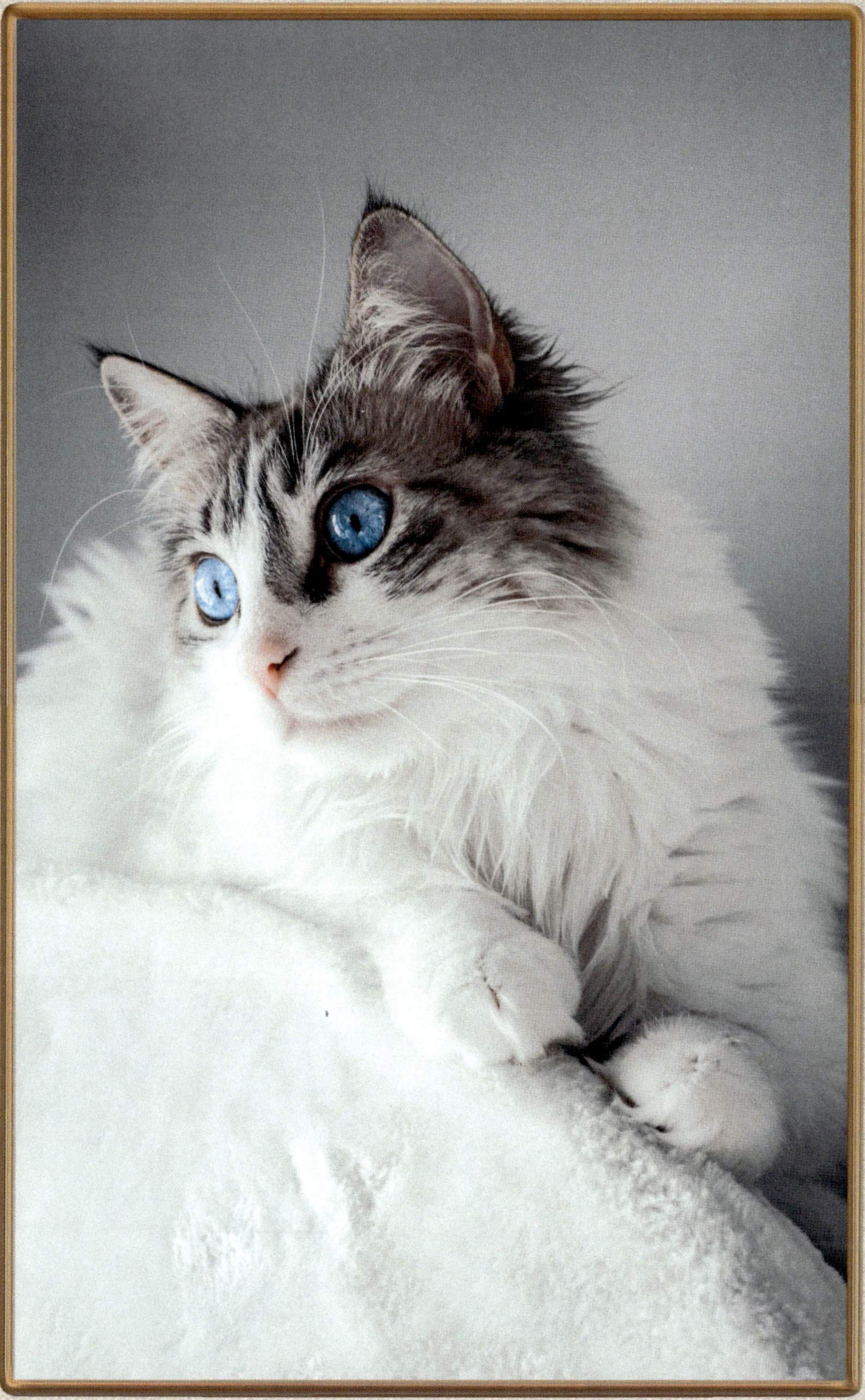

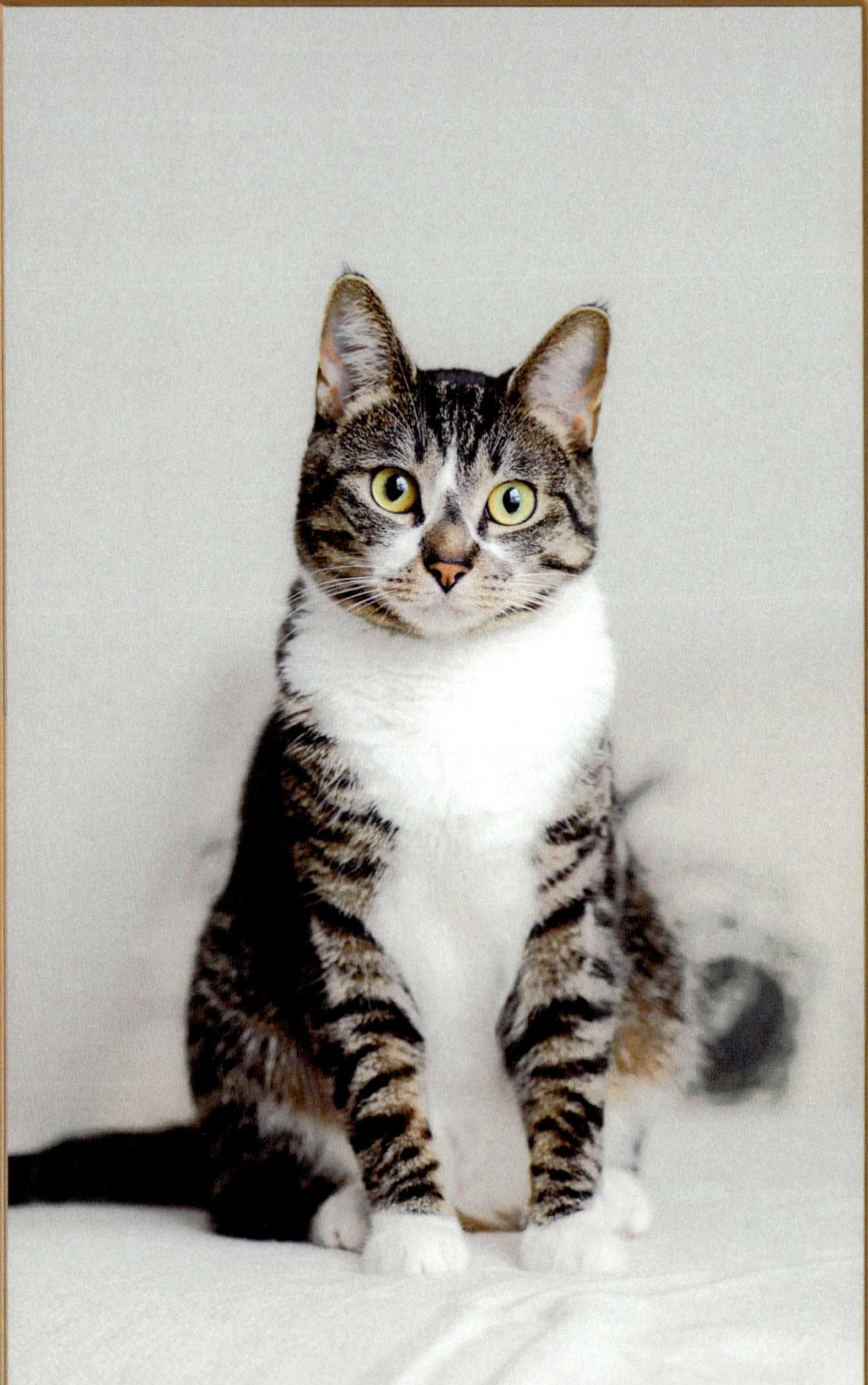

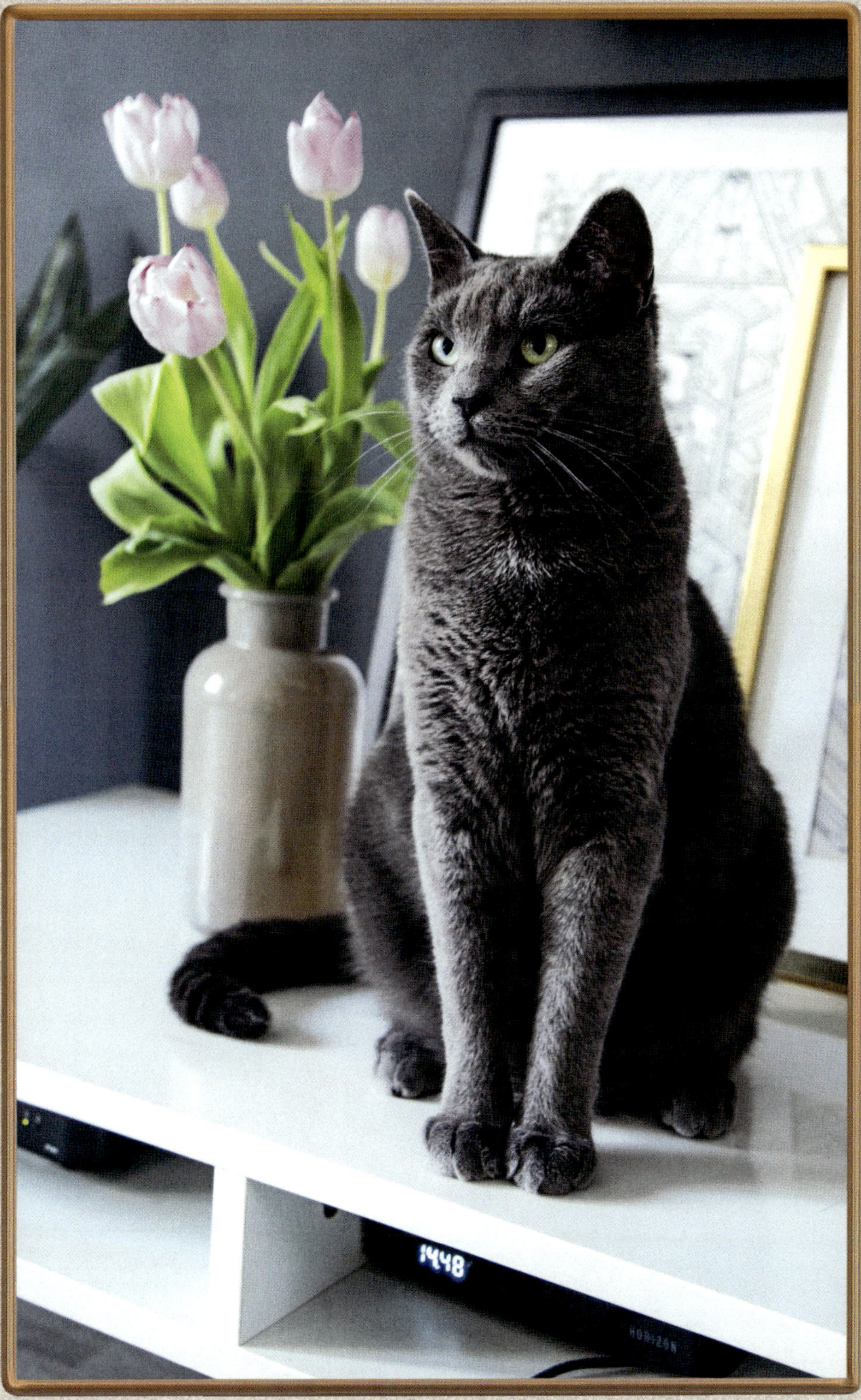
14:48

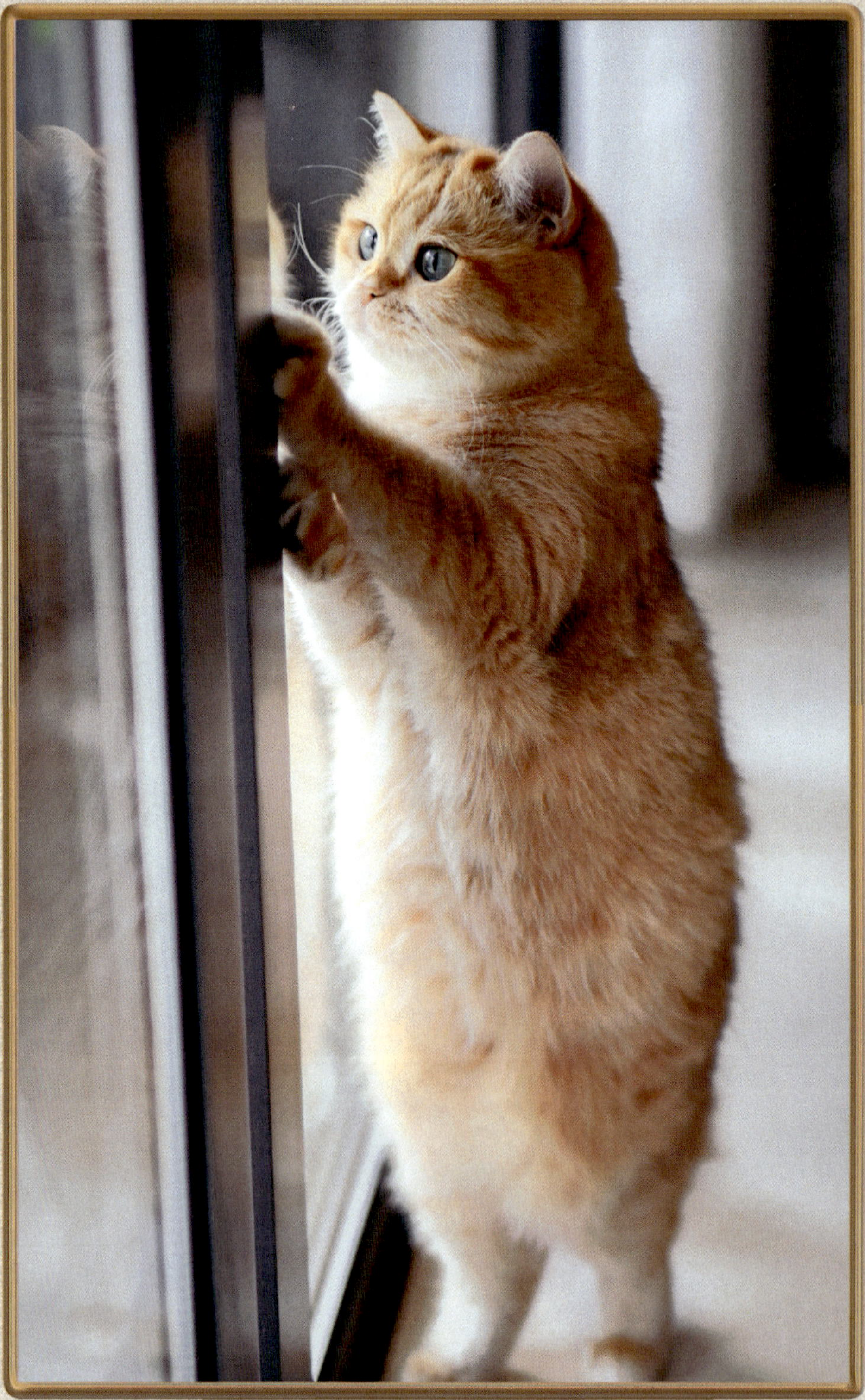

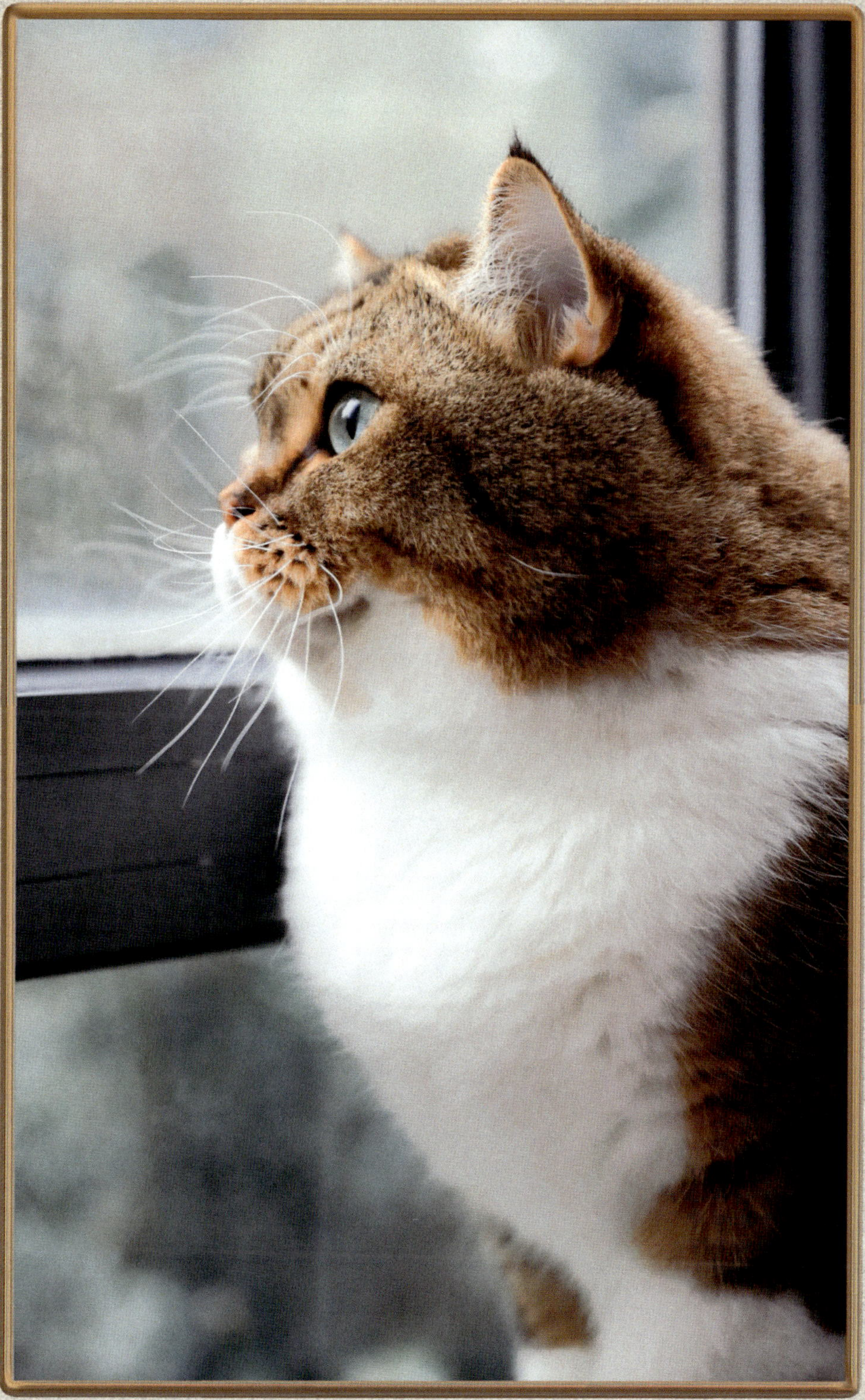

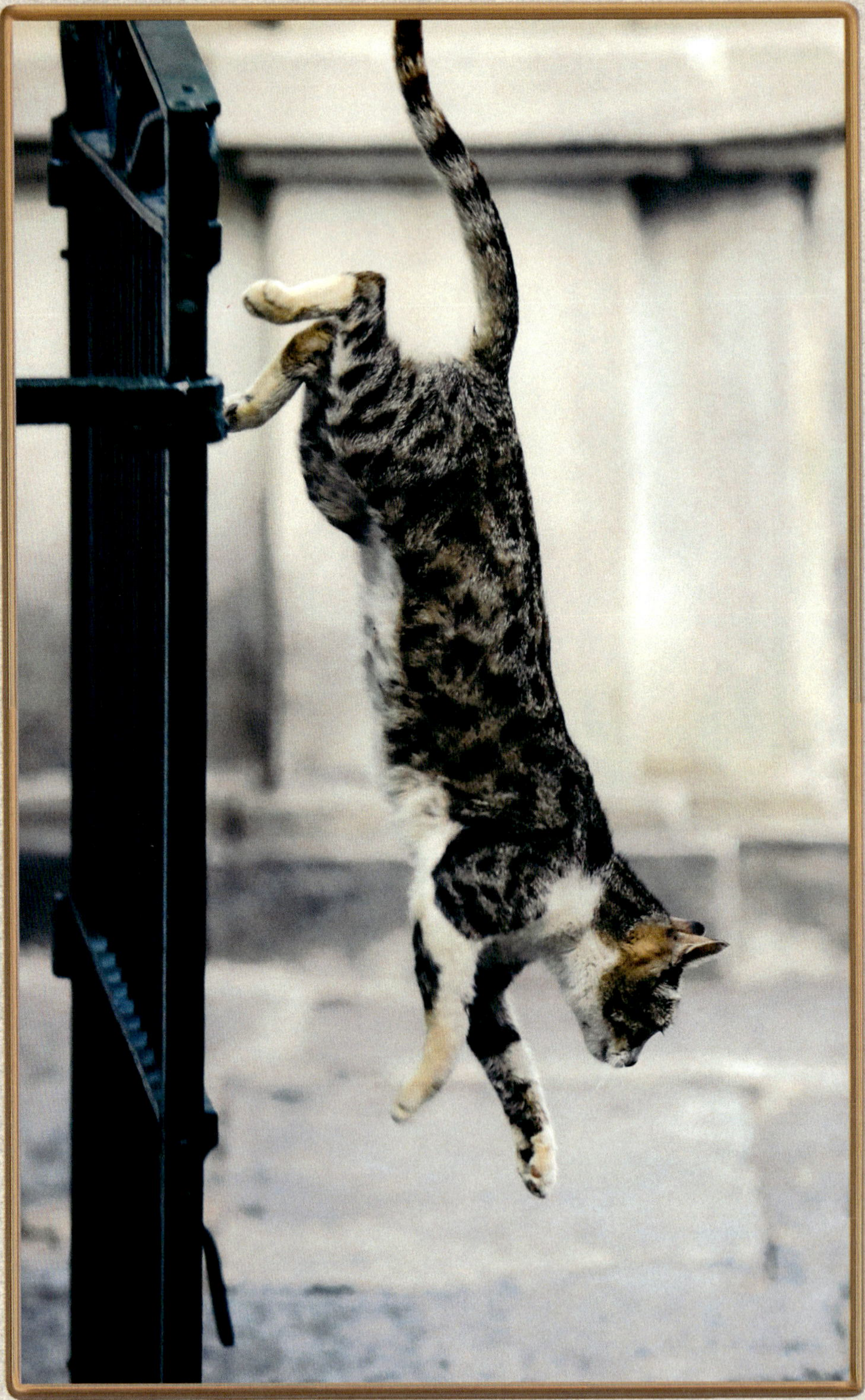

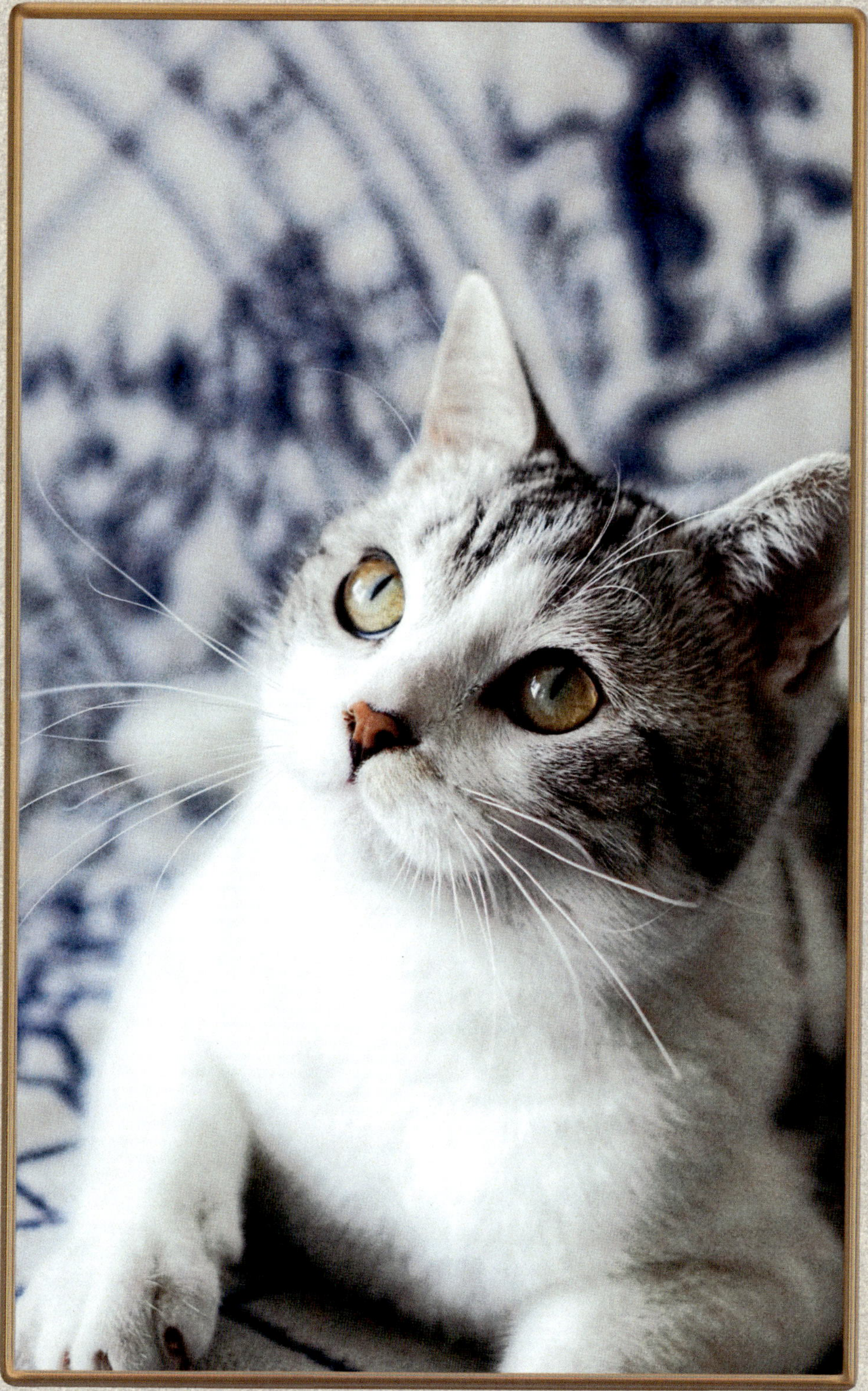

Manufactured by Amazon.ca
Bolton, ON

43821043R00026